Praise from Thought Leaders
for *Parents Who Lead*

"The intersection of working and becoming a parent can be daunting. Although what life-changing event is more magical than being a parent? In *Parents Who Lead*, Friedman and Westring offer wonderful stories, wisdom, and actionable advice about applying leadership principles at home. An inspiring read for working parents."

—**ARON AIN,** CEO, Kronos; author, *WorkInspired*

"I've been a champion of Total Leadership for over a decade, and its principles have been instrumental in my continued career success. *Parents Who Lead* applies these principles to the absolute toughest job—being a productive parent and role model—and it does not disappoint! Read this book, put it to practice, and see the results."

—**SAMUEL ALLEN,** SVP and COO, Marketing, Salesforce

"*Parents Who Lead* contains precious new knowledge for working parents. It's an engaging, science-based, essential guide to upgrading your life, financially supporting your family, and being a stellar parent. Friedman and Westring share an easy-to-follow, proven method to reduce your stress, succeed at work, and inspire your children to live healthy, meaningful lives."

—**DAVE ASPREY,** founder and CEO, Bulletproof; *New York Times* bestselling author, *Super Human*

"*Parents Who Lead* helps us prioritize, strategize, and take conscious action so we can lead more well-rounded, successful lives. Friedman and Westring share advice that is at once practical and inspirational. They are going to help a LOT of parents!"

—**SCOTT BEHSON,** Professor of Management, Fairleigh Dickinson University; author, *The Working Dad's Survival Guide*

"As a parent, a son, and a co-CEO, my main priority is to be present for—and create impact across—all the important relationships in my life. I know I share that goal with others living in a fast-paced digital world. *Parents Who Lead* makes that goal feel not only attainable but realistic."

—**NEIL BLUMENTHAL,** cofounder and co-CEO, Warby Parker

"*Parents Who Lead* encourages working mothers and fathers to take a crucial step back from their challenging day-to-day responsibilities to home in on the values that can transform their families. The enjoyable exercises are worth the time, as they can lead to more fulfilling relationships and careers and to happier children with brighter futures."

—**MEREDITH BODGAS,** Editor in Chief, *Working Mother*

"Every parent is a leader. Every parent experiences the challenge of having too much to do in precious and finite time. *Parents Who Lead* articulates a sustainable, manageable path forward through this often stress-inducing gauntlet to help us toward the realization of a well-lived and well-shared life."

—**SAM CALAGIONE,** founder and Brewer, Dogfish Head

"Parenting is the only 24/7 job that is legally allowed, and it's the most important job we ever do. Yet there is no training for it. *Parents Who Lead* is the ultimate guide that fills this void. A must-read for any parent!"

—**ZARJA CIBEJ,** CEO, myTamarin

"At last, an inspiring and informative book on one of the most challenging leadership issues of our time—parenting. *Parents Who Lead* is full of lessons on how to handle demands on your time and resources—at work, at home, and in relationships—while raising the next generation. Want to put everything in context and feel positive? Read this!"

—**MICHAEL DOWLING,** President and CEO, Northwell Health

"*Parents Who Lead* is a systematic, practical, and inspiring guide for parents who want to succeed in their careers and make the world better for their children. It's a crucial resource for organizations committed to attracting and retaining the best people who also happen to be parents."

—**ANNE ERNI,** Chief People Officer, Audible

"*Parents Who Lead* provides data-driven tools and pragmatic direction to those of us choosing to be exceptional leaders, both inside and outside our homes. This book is a must-read if you are a busy executive who wants to attain the highest possible ROI on the greatest investment of your life: your children."

—**JENNA FISHER,** Managing Director, Russell Reynolds Associates

"With *Parents Who Lead,* Friedman and Westring inspired me to go deeper with my wife, my children, and my community. If you're looking to strengthen the bonds with the people who matter most in your life, I highly recommend reading this book. It is well researched and heartwarming."

—**GREG FITZSIMMONS,** comedian and author

"Stew was one of my favorite Wharton professors, and his lessons have resonated with me as my wife and I raised our three boys and I built my health and wellness company into a five-hundred-person operation. This well-written, compelling book distills evidence-based wisdom into actionable, outcome-focused tasks destined to improve not just the parenting, but the lives of all who read it."

—**SHAUN FRANCIS,** Chair and CEO, Medcan; author,
Eat, Move, Think

"Stew Friedman and Alyssa Westring have applied their thoughtful, reflective, experiential approach to help us lead the lives we want in our families, careers, communities, and in staying healthy. If your life feels out of sync with what you want—and whose doesn't—this gift of a book is for you!"

—**ELLEN GALINSKY,** President, Families and Work Institute; author, *Mind in the Making*

"*Parents Who Lead* provides a formula for helping parents bring the principles of success from the workplace into their families, where leadership skills are often needed most. It's a wonderful blueprint for integrating work and the rest of life, a hallmark for defining success that sets the example for future generations."

—**ROBERT GLAZER,** CEO, Acceleration Partners; bestselling author, *Elevate* and *Performance Partnerships*

"The skills that define great leaders at work are surprisingly relevant to becoming a great parent at home. This book won't just help you identify those skills—it's a step-by-step guide for putting them into practice."

—**ADAM GRANT,** *New York Times* bestselling author, *Originals* and *Give and Take*

"In *Parents Who Lead*, Friedman and Westring bring together concepts too often separated—work and family, leadership and parenting—to the detriment of all. They integrate research with practical tools to help readers learn many enriching ways to improve their lives by focusing on the whole—their lives, careers, families, and communities."

—**BRAD HARRINGTON,** Executive Director, Boston College Center for Work and Family

"If struggling to meet work, family, and social demands means you feel too busy to read this book, then you *really* need to read it! It will help you unlock creative steps to live a more grounded, spacious, and fulfilling life. *Parents Who Lead* is a resource to draw on as your family and your career evolve."

—**GRACE HO,** Regional Lead, Women's Recruiting and Development (Asia), McKinsey & Company

"Working parents often feel doomed to do neither work nor parenting well. Friedman and Westring harness their experience as both leadership educators and parents to provide fresh insights for overcoming this common quandary. Read this book and learn how to lead your way into a new, more fulfilling, and successful way of parenting."

—**HERMINIA IBARRA,** Charles Handy Professor of Organizational Behavior, London Business School

"People increasingly feel that there's no point in succeeding at work only to fail at home. But what if they apply proven organizational leadership tools to their families? *Parents Who Lead* is a lively self-help book with a creative twist."

—**ROSABETH MOSS KANTER,** Harvard Business School Professor; author, *Think Outside the Building*

"Most leadership guides ignore the fact that many professionals are parents. *Parents Who Lead* provides a refreshing perspective on leadership, with practical tools for building a purpose-driven, rewarding life that embraces career and family. This book will help children, families, and working parents thrive!"

—**MOLLY KENNEDY,** Director, Dove Masterbrand US Engagement, Unilever

"Whether you're a new parent, or entering a different phase of your children's lives, or a grandparent, this book is for you. Stew Friedman has expanded his award-winning Total Leadership principles into a manifesto that is a game changer for the parenting and leadership literature."

—**STEPHEN K. KLASKO,** President and CEO, Thomas Jefferson University and Jefferson Health

"What a cool book! It spoke to me in so many ways. I needed this wisdom now, even after twenty-seven years of marriage and twenty-five years as an executive and mother of three. *Parents Who Lead* is a tremendous resource to refresh and increase the quality of our lives as partners, parents, and professionals."

—**LAURA KOHLER,** Senior Vice President, Human Resources, Stewardship, and Sustainability, Kohler, Co.

"*Parents Who Lead* offers useful exercises and concepts to help parents reflect and learn as a team how to create parenting partnerships and a collective vision for a better life. Readers will gain a new understanding of how to proactively align and enhance their parenting strategies."

—**ELLEN ERNST KOSSEK,** Basil S. Turner Professor of Management, Purdue University; former President, Work and Family Researchers Network

"Friedman and Westring masterfully translate social science evidence into practical steps for building the leadership capacity to cultivate our relationships with our children and with all those important to their development. The compelling examples will inspire parents of all ages to develop more meaningful lives, lived together."

—**SUSAN J. LAMBERT,** President, Work and Family Researchers Network; Associate Professor, University of Chicago

"It's fantastic to see a book that provides actionable, sensible, well-researched advice for both mothers and fathers. By focusing on parenting as a leadership challenge, *Parents Who Lead* empowers readers with a new way to make decisions that are best for their families and for themselves."

—**JOSH LEVS,** author, *All In*

"Stew Friedman does it again! Drawing on his groundbreaking *Total Leadership*, his evidence-based research reminds working parents and those who employ them that sustainable success means bringing your whole self to work. *Parents Who Lead* is brilliantly done—

a must-read guide that offers real solutions for working parents who strive to be values-driven leaders in today's fast-paced world."

—**DAVE LISSY,** Executive Chairman, Bright Horizons

"I have given Stew Friedman's books to hundreds of people. They are that good—best in category by a country mile! *Parents Who Lead*, with Alyssa Westring, draws on his entire lifetime of work. I only wish he had written it when I was just starting out as a parent."

—**F. WILLIAM MCNABB III,** former CEO, Vanguard

"I love this book! It's engaging, inspirational, and relatable. As the mother of a teenage daughter and the spouse of a physician husband, I identified with the parents in the book and was engrossed in their stories. *Parents Who Lead* is a great, timely resource for working parents and a landmark contribution to organizations seeking to embrace the whole lives of their employees."

—**JENNIFER H. MIERES, MD,** Senior Vice President, Center for Equity of Care and Chief Diversity and Inclusion Officer, Northwell Health

"Being a CEO is tough job, but it's not nearly as demanding as being a mom or a dad. Thank goodness, then, that Stew Friedman and Alyssa Westring have brought their knowledge of leadership to the challenge of parenting. *Parents Who Lead* will stir you to rethink your assumptions about yourself, your partner, and your kids—and map a more fulfilling future for your lives together. If you feel overwhelmed by the demands of work, family, and the rest of life, take back control with this insightful and compassionate book."

—**DANIEL H. PINK,** author, *When* and *Drive*

"In *Parents Who Lead*, Stew Friedman, who has been enlightening the Fatherly community since our inception, and Alyssa Westring have created a playbook for how leadership principles translate to hearth and home. It has already empowered me with tools for better communicating what I want for myself and from the relationships in my life."

—**MICHAEL ROTHMAN,** CEO, Fatherly

"It's hard to maintain a true parenting partnership, especially with a shared commitment to carry the mental and emotional load of leading your family together. Friedman and Westring provide a step-by-step plan for engaging your partner, children, colleagues, and community in building your family's life by design rather than by inertia."

—**MATT SCHNEIDER,** cofounder, City Dads Group

"I can think of no better guide than *Parents Who Lead* to help overwhelmed parents find time for what matters most. It's filled with compelling stories, evidence-based research, advice gleaned from the best of leadership science, and engaging, fun, and practical interactive tools. It's going to be so helpful to so many people."

—**BRIGID SCHULTE,** award-winning journalist; Director, Better Life Lab; author, *Overwhelmed*

"What a marvelous book! I wish I'd had it when I was a young parent, but it's equally valuable at the empty-nesting stage. The application of the Total Leadership approach to parenting is a wonderful reminder of how we can grow and lead in every area of our lives."

—**ANNE-MARIE SLAUGHTER,** CEO, New America

"*Parents Who Lead* is great! It offers a thoughtful approach to parenting, with tips for enriching and nurturing the most important relationships we have. This book is a must-read for every parent who seeks to transform not only their relationship with their children but their relationship with the world."

—**JULIE SMOLYANSKY,** CEO, Lifeway Foods

"*Parents Who Lead* is relentlessly engaging and useful for anyone who has children—or is considering becoming a parent. You, dear reader, won't think about either parenthood or leadership in quite the same way after your journey through Friedman and Westring's compelling blend of stories, advice, and practical exercises."

—**ROBERT SUTTON,** Organizational psychologist and Stanford professor; bestselling author, *Scaling Up Excellence, The No Asshole Rule,* and *Good Boss, Bad Boss*

"When you're both a mom and a leader, it can be confounding to have to manage a leadership dance. Finally, a book that treats parents like the leaders we are! *Parents Who Lead* provides real, not squishy, teachings and treats parents—especially moms, but dads too—with the respect we all deserve."

—**GENEVIEVE THIERS,** founder, Sittercity; Producer, *RUN the Series*

"I'm buying this book for my team and my clients. *Parents Who Lead* is a winning playbook for raising healthy children while pursuing our professional lives—and enjoying our lives in the process! It debunks the myth of "work/life balance" and shows us how to reimagine work and family as a mutual win."

—**SALLY THORNTON,** founder and CEO, Forshay

"Your children need you to read this profoundly useful book. Its practical insights will help you confront essential questions, make better everyday choices and learn how to lead a more enriched way of living—for you and your family. It's required reading for parents striving to earn an A+ in life."

—**TOM TIERNEY,** former Worldwide Managing Partner, Bain & Company; Chairman and cofounder, Bridgespan Group

"How do you manage a cross-country move and a new job while striving to be a great husband and dad for your two young children? Read this book to learn how to focus on *what* really matters with *who* really matters so you can lead with values at work and at home."

—**JASON TOFF,** Director of Product Management, Facebook

"Parents, whether they realize it or not, are leaders. Like the best leaders, they can unite people around a shared vision to achieve more than anyone can achieve alone. In this practical and encouraging book, Friedman and Westring guide parents toward creating a better life for their families and everyone around them."

—**LAURA VANDERKAM,** author, *Off the Clock* and *Juliet's School of Possibilities*

Praise from *Parents Who Lead* Workshop Participants

"Designed for busy working parents in an 'always on' digital world, this book is an engaging read filled with proven strategies, actionable advice, enlightening research, and real-life examples—including ours—from the life-transforming workshop we did with Stew and Alyssa. A must-read for career-driven leaders who want to be winning moms and dads."

—**DANIEL A. CHEN,** Head of Business Development, Quicken

—**LORETTA CHEN,** Corporate Controller, Paine Schwartz Partners

"The *Parents Who Lead* workshop provides a mind-opening, novel, and refreshing approach to leadership by upending the traditional notion of 'balance' and competing priorities. By following the steps, we learned how a single smart action can result in wins intertwining across all facets of our lives."

—**WES CHOU AND LISA CHUNG,** technology executives

"The *Parents Who Lead* program has been truly transformational. We were skeptical that we'd be able to make changes that would stick. But the concepts and structure came to life and yielded quick results, encouraging us to keep going to make meaningful, sustainable changes in our lives, with our children, and in our community."

—**DANA NAE GARCIA,** Executive, Vynamic

—**JAIME GARCIA,** Director, FS Investments

"We highly recommend the *Parents Who Lead* workshop! It helps you reflect on your core values and goals as a parent, and it's full of pragmatic ideas toward purposeful parenting. As we have practiced and incorporated these techniques into our lives together, we have become extremely close as a family."

—**ANJANA HARVE,** Chief Information Officer, Hillrom

—**ROHIT HARVE,** Pharma Life Sciences Operations Strategy Leader, Strategy&

"The *Parents Who Lead* workshop helped us bring the best parts of our professional lives—research, planning, structured communication, and experimentation—into our life at home. We had often drawn a line between who we are in our offices versus who we are in our personal lives. We acquired a tool set for breaking through those self-imposed barriers."

—**BLAINE MCLAUGHLIN,** FinTech executive

—**ANN THOMSON,** IT Operations executive

"We started the *Parents Who Lead* program during our busiest period as parents of two. It wasn't easy to find the time, but the immediate positive changes we saw urged us on. Now, with three children, busier than ever, we have the tools and confidence to stay the course toward achieving our vision for ourselves and our children."

—**LAURA D. RIVERA,** Global Finance Director, Johnson & Johnson

—**HON. MARC A. ALFARANO,** Magisterial District Judge

"This workshop provided us with specific strategies and a new vocabulary to parent with purpose, and to do so in a way that simultaneously enhanced our marriage, careers, and community relationships. It doesn't happen overnight, but we are living proof that *Parents Who Lead* can help you uncover solutions to some of parenting's truly daunting challenges."

—**LAUREN TANZER,** Cardiology Administrator, Children's Hospital of Pennsylvania

—**MATTHEW TANZER,** Managing Director, Bayada Strategic Ventures

Parents Who
LEAD

Parents Who
LEAD

The
Leadership Approach
You Need *to*
Parent with Purpose,
Fuel Your Career,
and
Create a Richer Life

STEWART D. FRIEDMAN
ALYSSA F. WESTRING

Harvard Business Review Press

Boston, Massachusetts

Library of Congress Cataloging-in-Publication Data

Names: Friedman, Stewart D., author. | Westring, Alyssa F., author.
Title: Parents who lead : the leadership approach you need to parent with purpose, fuel your career, and create a richer life / Stewart D. Friedman and Alyssa F. Westring.
Description: Boston : Harvard Business Review Press, [2020] | Includes index.
Identifiers: LCCN 2019041094 (print) | LCCN 2019041095 (ebook) | ISBN 9781633696501 (hardcover) | ISBN 9781633696518 (ebook)
Subjects: LCSH: Parenting. | Leadership. | Work and family. | Work-life balance.
Classification: LCC HQ755.8 .F748 2020 (print) | LCC HQ755.8 (ebook) | DDC 649/.1—dc23
LC record available at https://lccn.loc.gov/2019041094
LC ebook record available at https://lccn.loc.gov/2019041095

ISBN: 978-1-63369-650-1
eISBN 978-1-63369-651-8

The paper used in this publication meets the requirements of the American National Standard for Permanence of Paper for Publications and Documents in Libraries and Archives Z39.48-1992.

For our children

and their children and their children and their children . . .

May your songs always be sung.

Contents

List of Exercises

List of Tables

WHY WE WROTE THIS BOOK

We wrote this book to bring the science of leadership to the art of parenting. We want to help you lift your head up and out of the chaos and craft a way—together, with your family—to build something different, something that serves your career, your life as a parent, and your other aspirations in life. As researchers, educators, consultants, and coaches, we have decades of experience helping people learn how to succeed as they aim to have a positive impact in their work, in their communities, and at home—as leaders in all aspects of life. We know it can be better, and you can make it so.

In striving to be the parent you want to be, have a fruitful career, find time to nurture important relationships, engage as a citizen, and make sure you stay healthy and sane (and we know that doing all this is *very* difficult), you are not alone. Yet many parents worry that they're among the unfortunate few who haven't figured it all out. Through their work with us, they're happily surprised—relieved, really—to find that nearly *everyone* is struggling, albeit in their own distinct ways.

We've seen parents find greater harmony as well as better performance in all parts of their lives by viewing things in a new way. Observing how other parents wrestle with the demands of modern life, and how they apply our proven principles and tools, gives people both greater confidence and the resources to pursue the lives they want to lead. We expect this is what you're trying to do—forge a life that's fulfilling, creative, and meaningful for you, your family, your work, and your community. To make our research-based model available to you, so you can use it to make your world better, is our raison d'être. But there's a bit more to the story of why we produced this new leadership approach designed just for parents.

———————

From Stew: After getting my PhD in organizational psychology from the University of Michigan, my early career as a management professor at the Wharton School at the University of Pennsylvania was focused on understanding what makes effective leaders. After having my first child (over thirty years ago), however, I pivoted, as I viscerally realized something I had learned as a student from seminal scholars in my field: people don't just shelve the other parts of their lives when they are at work. I started talking about this with anyone who would listen.[1]

The idea of accounting for the whole person at work wasn't mainstream, either in business schools or in business culture, in the late 1980s and early 1990s, when much of the focus in the emerging field of work and life was, appropriately, devoted to women being supported in their quest to work outside the home in their chosen profession and be treated as equals to men at work. I became one of the accidental spokes*men* in a new conversation about work and life (italics added because, at the time, I was one of the few men interested in this topic). It's gratifying to see that there's been progress since those days. Yet it is undeniable that we still have a *long* way to go.[2] So I have continued to pursue practical knowledge for how to create harmony among the different parts of life in my research, teaching, consulting, and advocacy.

My students at the Wharton School, especially those in our executive MBA program, where I have been teaching the course that gave rise to this book for over fifteen years, have been clamoring for me to produce a guide for parents. So, this book is, in part, a response to their interest. But my motivation for working on this book stems even more profoundly from my family. My life partner, Hallie, and I have three children, now in their twenties and thirties. When I turned sixty-five a few years back, the only gift I asked for from these four precious people was this: write to me about what you'd like me to focus on in my remaining years and how, by my doing so, your life would be enriched . . . and be willing to talk this over for an hour, one-on-one. (Yes, the professor gave his family an assignment.) Among other things, they told me, each in their own way, how my research on parents applying leadership principles might help our family and be of some value to society. I came away from these conversations further inspired to write this book, for them and for you. But I needed a research partner and friend whose experience as a working mother (from a generation after mine) and knowledge as an accomplished scholar could inform what I might be able to say on my own.

———————

From Alyssa: By the time I graduated from college, I knew I wanted to dedicate my career to the science and psychology of helping people thrive in both their careers and personal lives. It is no coincidence I was passionate about this topic, considering I was already starting to fret about navigating my future career and raising my hypothetical children (this was more than a decade before I actually had them). While pursuing my PhD in organizational psychology at Michigan State University, my academic research was flourishing, but I longed to make an impact on people's lives. I searched for scholars doing this work on the front lines.

Stew's work was evidence-based and practical. I emailed him and asked if we could work together. In the thirteen years since, Stew has become a mentor and I have become director of research for our company, Total Leadership. My role is to determine what's working and what's not as we continually improve our model, which helps individuals and organizations create sustainable change that increases performance in all parts of life by finding greater harmony among them. As I became a tenured professor of management and entrepreneurship at DePaul University, we've continued to collaborate, culminating in this book. I've found a career path that allows me to bridge the gap between academic research and people's daily experience. I couldn't be happier about it.

At thirty-nine, I am a youngish working mom with two youngish kids, ages eight and ten. In fact, *Time* magazine interviewed me as a "millennial mom" for its cover story, "Help, My Parents Are Millennials." While I might not consider myself a millennial, I do feel connected with the challenges of being a working parent today. From learning that my mom was diagnosed with brain cancer just a week before starting my tenure-track job to my husband's unexpected stint as a stay-at-home dad, I've ridden the roller coaster of working parenthood and have amassed my own trove of epiphanies and embarrassing stories. I've been there. Rather, I am there. In fact, in one of the video interviews we did as part of our research for this book, my husband is chasing my naked daughter around our living room behind me while I try to remain focused. While there's no one right way, Stew and I can help you find what works for you and your family based on our own research, the scholarship in our field, and our experience working with clients and students, from undergraduates to executive MBAs.

———————

For the benefit of the world of today as well as the world of tomorrow, your children's world, you need to lead. We invite you to join us, to read on as we provide you with the tools we've developed so that you can achieve greater connection, engagement, and success—as *you* define it—in the modern world of 24/7 demands, the digital deluge, revolutionized gender roles, political tensions, and the increasing fragility of human existence on earth.[3]

Parents Who
LEAD

Chapter 1

THE LEADERSHIP CHALLENGE OF YOUR LIFE

Deena Altman and Jake Center met as fifteen-year-olds in summer camp, although they didn't start dating until their midtwenties, when they were living in New York City. After three years, they got married and now have two energetic boys, Ian, seven, and Casey, four. Jake is a practicing attorney in Charleston, South Carolina. He recently began studying Transcendental Meditation, but this doesn't eliminate the stress he feels as he tries to keep up at work and be present for his family. After college, Deena started a career in marketing, but she recently switched to nonprofit management, seeking work that felt more personally meaningful. Deena was one week into a busy new job as executive director of a nonprofit foundation and Jake was chugging steadily toward becoming a partner at his firm when we began our work with them.

On the surface, the big-picture stuff seemed to be going well. They both cared about their careers and about their relationships with each other and their children. As we got to know them, they confessed that they were constantly rushing, always playing catch-up, barely staying on top of their workloads, and struggling to squeeze enjoyment from their side-by-side lives. Jake put it this way: "When things are stressful at work, I feel even more overwhelmed at home. I can be short-tempered with Deena and the boys. I'll snap at them. I regret this. I don't like that work takes so much of my attention, but I don't see any way around it."

Deena faces daunting challenges, too, if a bit different: "Work distracts me at home and even when I'm in the car with Jake or with the kids—largely because of email, texts, and constant chirps from my stupid phone. I feel guilty that I'm not present enough for family, that I'm not a good mom, and that I need to pay more attention to my marriage. Even though I know better, I just can't seem to stop myself from jumping in when the latest crisis at work hits. I often feel disconnected from the very people I most want to feel connected to."

Sensing that their lives weren't what they wanted them to be, they agreed, though not without some trepidation, to participate in our workshop designed expressly for parents, based on the program described in Stew's book, *Total Leadership: Be a Better Leader, Have a Richer Life*. (See the box "Total Leadership and the Pursuit of Four-Way Wins.") Most of the people who join our workshops (some of whose stories are in this book—although names and other identifying information have been changed for privacy) have a similar sense of their lives barreling along, but that they're not in the driver's seat.

We were not surprised to find how many people in parenting partnerships feel as Deena and Jake do. (By parenting partnerships, we mean relationships of shared responsibility for raising children, which often means married couples, though not always.) Many people feel alone in their strife. They want things to be different, but they are mired in ways of thinking and acting that are no longer working and, as important, they don't believe there's a better way. They are not sure where to turn for advice on how to gain a greater sense of control and to create meaningful change.

You probably picked up this book because you too are feeling that you are not leading the life you really want as a parent. Perhaps you're just plain tired: tired of trying to coordinate busy work schedules with your parenting partner; tired of waiting for things to settle down; tired of feeling as if you aren't being your best self at work, in your most intimate relationships, and with your community of friends and extended family. And probably tired because you don't sleep enough. You are not alone. As parents, we've been there, too, and we've worked with people like you who have been there. Here are some of the things we hear from parents when we start working with them:

- I'm letting people down. My kids, coworkers, partner, and friends deserve better.

- There's not enough time for me to be the kind of parent I want to be.

- If I could just get my act together, I could have it all.

- I need to completely overhaul my life to make things work.

- I don't have control of my situation, so I can't really change the way things are.

- Other people don't understand what I'm going through. I'm really on my own.

- People are too busy to help me, and I don't want to bother them.

- My partner and I can't find much common ground on parenting.

- I'm not a leader.

If you're holding any of these assumptions, either consciously or not, you're bound to be undermining your own success. But our evidence shows that you can change your thinking and, by adopting leadership principles and tools, challenge assumptions, see your life in a new

Total Leadership and the Pursuit of Four-Way Wins

In the 2008 book *Total Leadership*, Stew introduced the idea of the "four-way win"—a new way of looking at the connections among the different parts of life and then taking action to improve performance at work, at home, in the community, and for yourself personally (mind, body, and spirit). This reframes the idea of "work/life balance," which implies sacrifice in one part for success in another.

It doesn't always have to be a zero-sum game.[1] Instead, the Total Leadership approach focuses on creating harmony, or integration, among all the aspects of our lives, which can be achieved by being real (acting with authenticity by clarifying what's important), being whole (acting with integrity by respecting the whole person), and being innovative (acting with creativity by continually experimenting with how things get done).

Evidence from studies of parents who have used this approach found that they significantly increase their satisfaction with their careers by 17 percent, with their family lives by 31 percent, with their community engagement by 39 percent, and with their personal well-being by 54 percent. Moreover, they report a 23 percent improvement in both their physical and mental health as well as a 31 percent reduction in stress.

If you've read *Total Leadership*, you might recognize some of the basic principles in the pages that follow, but they're applied in a new way here. If you're not familiar with *Total Leadership*, don't worry. We'll supply the fundamentals, redesigned to help parents meet the leadership challenges they face. In this book, we will show you, as a parent, how to take the four-way view of your world, systematically observing your life as a whole rather than as an endless series of trade-offs. You'll form a new appreciation for how no one part exists in isolation, so you can make better decisions about how to invest your most precious asset—that is, your attention. You'll get smarter about how to manage boundaries between, for example, work and family.

Taking the four-way view will give you fresh insights about how work, family, community, and your private self all affect each other, in your life and in your partner's, too. You'll then generate practical, exciting ideas for your family to pursue four-way wins—customized by you to fit sustainably in your world.

Like *Total Leadership*, this book is not about survival tactics or life hacks but is instead a proven guide for building lives of significance, with the emphasis here on what it means to do so if you're a parent. The method we describe and illustrate gets results because there is no one best way, no "one size fits all," no fixed prescription. What *is* required is to consciously choose what matters, connect with who matters, and create innovative ways to make things better.

way, and find greater harmony and better performance in all aspects of your life.

Drawing on the scientific literature in psychology, sociology, and leadership studies, we've developed a leadership approach that is specifically designed for parenting partnerships in which the members have careers, whether or not both are currently employed outside the home.

We have found that developing as a leader has much in common with growing as a parent. The process of creative change starts with you. It just might be that the way you think about parenting and its place in your life is holding you back. Through the activities we lay out here, some of which you will undertake alone and some together with your partner in parenting, you'll come to see that your assumptions about what it takes to perform well in all your life's roles, especially as a parent, might be misguided. Through discovery, dialogue, and design of new ideas, we'll guide you to systematically take actions that will enable you to test these assumptions and, if you become aware of how they're causing unnecessary frustration or even failure, to alter them.

While we can't make everything easy, perfect, and without some sacrifice, we'll show you how to explore the values that unite you, the passions that drive you, and the vision you hold collectively for the future—for your children. We'll provide you with tools you can use to define success on your own terms, connect more meaningfully with people in your life, and try innovative ways to nurture your career, your family (however you define it), your community, and your personal well-being.

Parent with Purpose, Fuel Your Career, and Create a Richer Life

It might not seem obvious at first, but raising children is a leadership challenge, perhaps the most important one you'll ever face. Being a parent requires seemingly endless amounts of energy and patience, illuminates our shortcomings, and mystifies us at every turn. As we try to lead our children toward happy, compassionate, and confident lives, we must figure out how to do so while at the same time investing in what matters most to us elsewhere in life.

At some point on the journey with us, most of the parents in our workshops feel a jolt; the realization that as parents they *are* indeed leaders, capable of mobilizing others toward a goal that matters, and that growing as a leader isn't just about work—it's about life.[2] Whether or not they are in an official leadership role at work, they realize they have the capacity to inspire. Rather than seeing themselves as mere administrators of their lives, reactively overseeing to-do lists, they start to view themselves as leaders who are consciously designing an achievable future—the one they truly want—and showing the people around them how to make that feast a reality they can savor together.

Our goals are to educate and to provoke, to push you to think of yourself as a leader and act like one, but not in the traditional sense of having formal authority, or of being in charge of people in an organizational hierarchy or political setting. Leaders are those who see how to improve things and inspire people to pursue a better future together.

Let's now take a more detailed look at the leadership approach we'll explore in this book. In the chapters that follow, we'll describe the actions you can take, on your own and then together as a partnership. (Most people find it takes a few months to methodically work through the book's activities, in light of the other responsibilities in their lives.) You'll articulate what really matters, build trust and strengthen relationships with your most important people, and develop creative ways to be more of who you want to be.[3] We'll explain what we want you to do and why. Along the way, we'll dive into the stories of some of the parenting partnerships, people like Deena Altman and Jake Center, who have teamed up with us to increase their dexterity in working together to parent with purpose and find greater harmony. We expect you'll see some of your own experience reflected in these stories, and this will help you compose your own stories about the adventures you have in learning to live in closer accord with your values.

Envision Your Future Together

A leader has a vision of a future that's better than today. To get excited about changing in meaningful ways, you need to be able to vividly picture what you want your life to look like. You might find it easy to do that, though not everyone does. And when your life is intertwined with others, the challenge is greater, as it becomes envisioning a future that you, your partner, *and* your children want. This vision should allow each of you the flexibility to pursue your individual passions and fulfill your most important values, while uniting you in shared dreams.

You'll come together to create what we call a "collective vision," to align and start to see new interconnections between one another and among various domains of your lives. We'll guide you through the inevitable challenges that arise when you realize that your dreams and your partner's may not be entirely in sync, and we'll help you learn how to get to common ground. We'll advise you on defining the path you want to walk together and on seeing how, in your everyday life on that path, you serve as a role model for the next generation. No two visions are alike. We'll not presume to prescribe what yours should be; rather, we'll help you see the power of crafting yours *together* and using it as a guide, starting now.

Embrace the Four-Way View

To move toward your vision together, you need to take an honest look at how things are now. In order to do so, you'll take the four-way view and notice how the different parts of your life are interconnected. Taking stock of how happy you are and how well you're performing in the different aspects of your life serves as a powerful and practical motivator—it moves you to make changes and not just mindlessly maintain the status quo.[4] But not only do you need to reflect on your own life, you need to candidly communicate at least some of this information with your partner, children, and other important people. Even our friends and family members don't always grasp how we're feeling about the different parts of our lives, and how important these arenas are to us.

Revealing a full picture of our lives sometimes means getting honest about the darker side of parenting—like guilt, fear, or the disappointing fact that sometimes parenting isn't quite the fulfilling endeavor we were told it should be. But effective leaders don't hide from reality because it's uncomfortable or inconvenient. You will gain the self-awareness you need to understand yourself in new ways and so communicate more genuinely and compassionately, for your own benefit and that of your key relationships.

Engage Your Children

We expect you will be surprised to learn just how much, and what, your children have to say about your lives together.[5] We'll help you begin age-appropriate dialogues about the values essential to your family and the vision of your future together. You'll uncover some of the crucial messages you are implicitly and explicitly sending to your children, some of which you may want to revise. And you'll enrich the quality of your connection with your children by drawing them closer.

Beyond that, you'll get to hear their creative, often dumbfounding, and sometimes downright hilarious suggestions about what you might try together as a family. One single father in our research, Dominic Martin, discovered that his four-year-old son, Leo, desperately wanted Dominic to teach him how to do new things. When Dominic inquired further, it turned out that Leo specifically wanted to learn how to vacuum! Not only were they able to identify a shared value (learning new things together), but Dominic got some newfound help with household chores, freeing up a bit of time for other things. You may be surprised to learn that your children don't necessarily need or want you to spend a lot more time with them. Rather, they may want you to put away your phone and your to-do list and just be present, both physically *and* psychologically. Doable but head-turning ideas can emerge when you open channels of communication and enlist your children in making changes.

Connect with Colleagues

For many of us, work not only is a source of income, but also shapes our identity. Our careers affect our self-confidence, inform our sense of purpose, and enable our social affiliations.[6] Despite the central role of work in our lives, though, many of us don't dedicate much time to thinking proactively about when, where, or how we work. We often assume that our conditions of work are set in stone and that the only way to survive is to adjust everything *other* than work to accommodate its demands. We cut sleep, relaxation, time with our children, all in deference to what we think is expected from us in our careers and from our colleagues. For some of us, unpredictable and grueling hours are unavoidable. For many of us, though, they just *seem* unavoidable. Our research has revealed practical ways to make changes at work that improve our lives outside work *and* allow us to be more productive in our jobs. But those opportunities for change need to be unearthed. No one gives them to us.

Bosses, colleagues, subordinates, clients, investors, former coworkers, and mentors are all part of the web of people who can help us succeed as parents. When people talk about the connection between work and family, they often articulate a "leave your personal life at the door" approach. But we are all who we are, no matter where we are. And who we are in our careers affects our children's lives, including their emotional health.[7] We will show you how to strengthen the relationships central to your career so that you have a network of colleagues who want to see you thrive at work, but also outside of work, especially as a parent.

Cultivate Your Community

An ancient, oft-repeated proverb says that "it takes a village" to raise a child. But what you may not often hear is how to build and keep that village in these modern times. Too many working parents feel disconnected from all but a few people in their work and home lives. In order to succeed as a family, you need to get other people on board—community members, caregivers, friends, and extended family—and to do so in a way that makes them feel good about their relationship with you. You probably feel, like most working parents, that you don't have enough time to invest in any more relationships. But we'll show you how building your village brings you not only a sense of belonging, community, and connection, but also genuine support. The investment is worth it.

You'll learn to shift how you think about relationships—each of you on your own and together as a partnership—and you'll begin to identify opportunities to strengthen existing relationships so they tap into new areas of your life, bringing tangible benefits. If you're like most people we have seen grow through this process, you will feel replenished as you better understand the support that's actually available to you in your world.

Try a New Way

It's common to feel trapped in chains of our own making; we often fail to note how one part of life affects the others and so miss opportunities to find the freedom to make things better when we learn to see the whole and act to change it. It's more fruitful to think of a pool rather than a prison, and to see how a pebble thrown into the pool ripples out, over time, affecting all the roles we play. You'll learn to see interconnections between your family, career, community, and personal lives. We'll help you uncover opportunities to improve the performance and well-being of all those in your family. Smart experiments you'll plan together will revitalize your world.

We'll tell you stories of families—some we expect may be much like yours—who were skeptical that they could change how they face the demands of the different parts of their lives. We'll share with you what they tried, what worked, and what they learned, especially when things didn't turn out as planned. We'll help you grasp the power of small wins and how to use them to leap forward as leaders, as a parenting partnership, and as a family.

See Yourself Differently

As a result of all of this reflection, conversation, and experimentation, you'll begin to view yourself differently. You'll come to see yourself leading in ways you have not before. Instead of feeling as though you are just surviving, barely keeping your head above water, you will see yourself going strong, like a skilled swimmer in life's waters.

We'll help you reflect on what you've learned—and how you've grown—to solidify your parenting partnership as something like a leadership team. We hope you find yourself fueled by your mutual commitment to a shared future, capable of continual growth, and able to inspire others along the way—your children, of course, but also your colleagues, neighbors, extended family, caregivers, and friends. We'll teach you how to keep the momentum going after you've read this book, inspiring those around you to continuously reflect, connect, and learn together.

Get Started

The ideas we're about to teach you are straightforward guidance for creating meaningful, sustainable change. The tough part is actually investing the time to work through these steps thoughtfully, interactively, and openly. Go at your own pace but avoid the temptation to rush through the exercises. Find a way to write or record your responses to them that works for you. You can access helpful resources at www.ParentsWhoLead.net.

Being parents who lead requires both individual and collective thought and action. Any strong partnership begins with individuals who have well-founded ideas and aspirations. The challenge—the fun and creative part—is bringing your ideas together. We'll ask you to do this in each chapter after you've prepped separately, to make something new that neither could do without the other. On your own, together, on your own, together—that's the weave. That's the sequence we recommend.

We are confident it'll be worth your while. Take it from another of our workshop participants, Lily Conrad, a project manager, practicing Buddhist, and mother to three-year-old Zainah. We asked her for advice she'd give to you, as a reader of this book, and here's what she said: "You're going to think this is a really big pain in the ass, and there is some pain, but the outcome and the results are phenomenal. All of the difficulty that you have, figuring out who you are and what you value, and figuring out who your partner is and then connecting, is all worth it at the end."

Reflecting, writing, and talking to each other, as we recommend, can seem like a big inconvenience added to already strenuously busy lives. It takes time, it forces you to recognize some truths about yourselves and your lives, and it may lead to some difficult conversations. But there's benefit to be gained from intentionally disrupting the status quo. (See the box "Identify Your Own Goals," and follow the instructions.)

Before we ask you to share your goals with your partner in parenting, let's review some guidelines for working together as a team—and enjoying it. You might actually find it exciting, and quite possibly romantic. Of course, it will probably be frustrating at times, too.

Do your level best to avoid making assumptions about what your partner *really* means, wants, or needs. It's often those partners who have known each other the longest who gain the most from these

IDENTIFY YOUR OWN GOALS

The very first step is for you, as an individual, to think and jot down what you hope to get out of reading this book and doing the exercises we offer. Write down your responses to the prompts so you can refer back to them later and then share them with your partner. Find a quiet spot and take ten minutes to compose your responses:

1. We know you're busy, so why take time out of your schedule to do these things? What's in it for you? For your children? For your career? For your important relationships? In other words, in an ideal world, how would you think, feel, and act differently after reading this book?

2. What about this book are you most looking forward to?

3. What's your greatest source of dread?

conversations because they're so used to speaking in shorthand and rarely stop to challenge their assumptions. Ask thoughtful questions and encourage your partner to explain thoughts and feelings more deeply. Then listen. By doing so, you not only improve your understanding of each other but deepen your understanding of yourselves. These are critical conditions for lasting growth.

You don't need to agree with everything your partner says or does. We can pretty much guarantee you won't. You can have different goals, values, and approaches and still work together to support one another as parents and in your separate lives. Speak compassionately and respectfully to one another and realize that these potentially difficult conversations are important steps in moving toward the future you want. (For more guidance before undertaking this initial conversation, check out the last section in chapter 3, "Understand Each Other's Needs.")

Be smart about how you work together. Use what you already know about each other to find what works best for you in how you take up the exercises we prescribe. Some partners find that reading each other's writing in the activities enables a more carefully considered exchange of ideas. Others prefer to just talk it out. Some find that having these conversations in the evenings after the children are asleep offers a serene opportunity for connection; others find they're too tired and cranky late at night.

You are the experts on you. Don't be afraid to try out different ways of approaching this book, both on your own and with your partner. Working together, coaching each other, as opposed to doing this sort of work on your own, makes it much easier to get unstuck, to move in

IDENTIFY YOUR SHARED GOALS

Share your goals for participating in this work with your parenting partner. Once you've done so, specify both the shared *and* the unique reasons each of you wants to do this project by writing responses to these questions:

1. What are the things you have in common as goals for this venture?

2. What goals are unique to each of you?

3. What did you discover by discussing your goals for the journey ahead?

a direction you want to go, because you can provide both support and accountability pressure (in a good way) for each other. (See the box "Identify Your Shared Goals.")

Find the Right Support

We have a few more comments to set the stage before you go further. We are organizational scholars, experts in the fields of both leadership and the relationship between work and the rest of life. We are parents. But we are not marriage counselors, although Stew did work with families in the seventies when he was studying clinical psychology and training as a therapist. Nor are we pediatricians, child guidance counselors, or early education specialists, though we do address directly the physical and mental health needs of children, drawing in part on research Stew conducted in one of the few studies on the impact of parents' careers on the emotional health of their children.[8]

We'll provide you with research-based guidance on what we know, but if specific challenges unique to your family emerge that require the expertise of a specialist, we encourage you to seek out their support. There is no shame in seeking help, of all kinds; indeed, doing so can and, we believe, should be a source of pride. And it will serve as a good model for your children that it's OK to acknowledge problems and to ask for help.

In addition to professional support, we encourage you to be on the lookout for parents who might like to join you on this journey of reflection, conversation, and growth—perhaps to see them as part of your intentional community. In our work with parents, we've found that a useful element in the staying power of positive change is the support of other parents. In our workshops, we create coaching exchanges, matching parents with one another to read each other's writing, provide feedback, maintain accountability, and share experiences and ideas. It's a good idea to create your own coaching exchange by finding other parents who might like to participate in the journey alongside you. The appendix offers more on the many ways a coaching exchange can be useful, how to launch one, and what to do—and *not* do—to ensure its successful growth.

This book is geared to couples, with some of the exercises to be done by each member alone, and some by the pair. (It can be read by just one partner and not the other, though it's more useful when done so together.) Many single parents have partners in parenting who are not their marital or romantic partners; they might be close friends, extended family members, childcare providers, their own parents (that is, their children's grandparents), and others. If you are a single parent, you might discover, from the exercises we ask you to do, that you're not as alone as you might have thought. You'll be strengthening important relationships not only in your immediate family but also in your extended family, in your job and career generally, and in your friendships and with others in your community. But if, as a single mother or father, you conclude that you are truly on the parenting journey on your own, you might find the more individually focused approach described in *Total Leadership* to be more relevant for your lifestyle.

Most of the parents with whom we've worked, and about whom you'll read in this book, are professionals who are in heterosexual marriages. We try to also address some distinctive experiences, gathered as part of our research, of people who don't fit this type of family structure—gay couples, divorced co-parents, single parents, and couples in which one parent is not working outside the home. But we believe our approach works for parents not just in particular kinds of relationships and not just in particular social milieus or work contexts. Our method is designed to be customized to fit everyone's unique situation, so it works whether you live in a city, in the suburbs, in the exurbs, in a small town, or on a farm, and whether you work in a large corporation or a small mom-and-pop shop, in the business world or in education, medicine, the arts, government, the trades, or a nonprofit organization.

Most of the partnerships we've studied cope with the demands of work and the rest of life by operating on autopilot. When you're on autopilot, reacting to whatever's next, it's easier to coast along, accepting the status quo, rather than to stop and question how and why you're doing things. Throughout this book, we're going to push you to turn off the autopilot and to rethink your assumptions about yourself, your partner, your children, and your lives together.

You might find yourself resisting opportunities to see or do things in different ways. When you feel that resistance bubbling up inside, remind yourself that this means you are doing something right. If everything you do in this book feels easy and comfortable, you probably won't get much out of it. Indeed, you're probably just skimming the surface. So, when the jitters come, remember what we're telling you right now: your willingness to be vulnerable is your superpower, not your kryptonite. It frees you to explore the principles and tools in this book with an adventurous spirit, an open heart, and compassion for the struggles of others.

We know from our work with thousands of people around the world that it helps to think of yourself as a scientist seeking new knowledge. Your passionate curiosity will help you get the most out of this book. Your children stand to benefit from changes that result from you deliberately trying to make things better. And they'll be learning from you as you model for them what it takes to lead your life with intention.

PART I

YOUR PARTNERSHIP

Chapter 2

ENVISION YOUR FUTURE TOGETHER

To lead our families into the future, we need to have an idea of where we want to go and why we want to go there. Not coincidentally, this is the sine qua non of leadership.

Rachel and Josh Steiner are full-fledged city people living in downtown Chicago with their two children, Samuel, going on three, and Ethan, ten months old. We asked Rachel and Josh to travel in time fifteen years into the future and describe, vividly and specifically, an ideal day.[1] This is what they wrote:

> On a Thursday in February, fifteen years from now, our alarm clock wakes us at 6:30 a.m. We hop on "his and hers" spin bikes and crank out thirty-minute rides. Our four kids, three biological and one adopted, are all old enough to get up on their own, get dressed, and make themselves breakfast. After they leave for school, we enjoy breakfast together before walking to our offices in the Loop. Rachel heads to a fast-growing health-care consulting startup, where she is chief operating officer. She is in and out of meetings all day, working closely with other senior

leaders while finding time to mentor one or two promising senior managers. Josh heads to the medical center, where he was recently promoted to senior vice president and chief innovation officer, following in the footsteps of one of his early mentors. Josh reviews several research grant proposals and approves an investment in cutting-edge medical technology.

After work, we divide and conquer on a busy evening of activities for the kids. Rachel watches the older boys play on the same basketball team. Josh leaves the office at 4 p.m. to swing down to watch the younger kids perform in a play with their Hebrew school. He feels a swell of pride seeing how important Judaism is to his kids. Everyone gets home by 7:30 p.m., and we sit down for a healthy meal together. After dinner, the kids wrap up their homework and go off to bed. At 9:00, we both jump on conference calls for the nonprofit boards we sit on. By 10:30, we retire to the bedroom where it's lights-out and some cuddling (wink, wink) after another busy yet immensely satisfying day as a family.

In some ways, this perfect picture of their lives fifteen years from now doesn't resemble their present lives. Today, they're chasing after two children in diapers; their future vision describes four relatively self-sufficient teenagers. Today, they can each barely squeeze in a workout or two a week, and they haven't done any volunteer work since having babies; in their ideal future, they're waking up and exercising together and serving on the boards of multiple charities.

In other ways, though, this vision echoes their lives right now. Rachel and Josh don't imagine moving to the suburbs or buying a yacht. They envision that they will still work in the same professions and industries, albeit in more senior positions. Josh sees himself continuing to ride the spin bike regularly. In the future, Rachel joins him. Yet writing this vision together had a powerful impact on Rachel and Josh and invigorated them. Rachel brought it up over coffee with friends. Josh described it to a coworker at lunch. It heightened their sense that they were working toward something bigger as a partnership rather than merely surviving the day-to-day chaos of working while raising young children. And they couldn't wait to start making changes in their lives that would move them closer to this vision.

We're going to walk you through the process Rachel and Josh undertook to come up with this image of their collective future. We'll break this process down into a few discrete steps so that you can end up with a vision that inspires you, motivates you, and guides your family. We'll warn about potential land mines and how to avoid them. We're *not* going to focus on the many ways dreams can be dashed by outrageous fortune, because the purpose here is not to plan for all contingencies in the next fifteen years.[2] Rather, it's to express, as an aspiration, what you really care about right now.

As we said in the first chapter: it's not easy, but it's *so* worth it.

Value Values

Before you and your partner can compose your vision together, you have to describe your values, the things that matter most to each of you. Values, it turns out, are the foundation on which a vision is built.

Personality researchers define values as "stable broad life goals that are important to people."[3] Let's break that definition down into its constituent parts. First, *stable* implies that your values may evolve but they aren't likely to dramatically shift over the course of your adult life. Second, they are *broad*, not tied to specific times, people, places, or outcomes (*going skydiving* is a goal, but *adventure* is a value). A third feature is what this definition *doesn't* include, namely, your behaviors. Values don't describe how you currently act. They describe what you think is important, even if it might not be obvious based on your actions. You might value cherishing the earth and all its precious creatures while not actively devoting time and attention to this.

Understanding and then communicating core values is a fundamental step in becoming an inspiring organizational leader.[4] Similarly, shifting from reactive parenting toward inspired parenting requires a commitment to discovering core values. Theories about transformational leadership, authentic leadership, ethical leadership, and servant leadership—to name but a few types—all consider a leader's transmission of values to be a central component.[5] Leaders who are aware of their values, convey them clearly, and act in alignment with them are engaged, generate high performance, and inspire commitment in their followers.[6] Think of any famous scene from a movie in which someone who is asserting leadership—a coach, a shop-floor employee, or a corps commander like Henry V—inspires a group in dire straits to overcome the odds and emerge victorious. How do they do this? Chances are that the person identified a few core values—"This is who we are and this is what we stand for!"—spurring the unlikely heroes to perform beyond reasonable expectation.

Why is awareness of values so essential to effective leadership? When we are aware of our values, we are able to make conscious choices about our actions that align more closely with those values. In doing so, we radiate confidence, communicate more clearly what matters most to us, and inspire others. Just as our children want a better answer for why they should behave in a certain way than "because I said so," when we understand our values, we can make thoughtful choices and communicate those choices much more effectively.

As parents with careers, why would we make our decisions based on anything other than what matters to us? While our values are shaped during our upbringing—by parents, schools, and religious institutions—many of us do not stop and reflect on them as adults and determine whether these are the values we want to embrace and, ultimately, transmit to our own children.[7]

As adults, too, we are constantly absorbing, and in some cases internalizing, the values of our coworkers, neighbors, partners, and friends.

Yet this is often as much unconscious as it is conscious. Social media, for example, can amplify the impact of comparisons with others, making it harder to stay centered, to know ourselves. When we see a cousin post a sweaty after-workout selfie, we think, "I need to be working out every day." When a former colleague posts about his latest career move, we think, "Why am I still stuck in the same job?" When an Instagram influencer posts pictures of her child's hand-crafted birthday party, with homemade decorations and food, we think, "I'm a lazy, unimaginative parent." Whether we realize it or not, these comparisons shape our definition of what "success" looks like, and it can nudge us toward implicitly adopting others' values, rather than solidifying our own.[8] Conversely, when our values are consciously identified, clarified, and expressed, we can more easily challenge insidious inner monologues about what we *should* be like. We can use what we truly care about as the basis for making decisions, both small and large.[9]

I (Alyssa, one of the authors), despite spending countless hours writing and speaking about values, recently fell into the "compare and despair" trap myself. I saw on social media that a graduate school classmate was promoted to dean of a prestigious business school. Almost immediately, I started to question why I wasn't even close to being a dean. I considered that I might be too complacent, that I derailed my career by having children, and that I just wasn't "dean material." Fortunately, I've gotten pretty good at focusing on *my* values and reminding myself of *my* definition of success. I had a conversation with myself about how deans have to manage budgets, oversee policies, and fundraise. I have no interest in those things and instead value helping people through my research, something deans have little time to do. In this way I was able to talk myself out of this feeling that I had somehow gone off track by telling myself, by reminding myself, that that was never the track I wanted. But, for someone less versed in articulating her own values and using them to define success on her terms, this could lead not simply to feeling bad about herself and her career trajectory, but perhaps to something worse; climbing a career ladder she doesn't even want to be on or getting so down on herself that she sabotages her success on her chosen path. By clarifying our values, we are better able to avoid the trap of benchmarking our success against others'; we can stay true to who we want to be even when the temptation to diverge strikes.

To spur your thinking as you consider your own values—the values that you aspire to embody in your career, parenting, and the rest of life—here are examples of values listed by parents in our research.

Achievement: A sense of accomplishment or mastery. I always strive to be the best that I can be and I respect others who do the same.

Adventure: New and challenging opportunities, excitement, risk. I'm an entrepreneur at heart.

Collaboration: Close, cooperative working relationships, being part of a team.

Courage: A willingness to stand up for beliefs and to do the difficult thing despite any fears.

Generosity: The one thing for which I hope I am remembered when I pass from this earth is my generosity—of spiritual and physical means.

Humor: The ability to laugh at myself and at life.

Love: I can't imagine that anyone in the world is happier than I am when my kids run up to give me a hug after work.

Responsibility: My father was an alcoholic. As a result, I grew disappointed because of broken promises. Now, as an adult, I try to do what I say I will do, always.

Spirituality: I'm a Catholic and believe there is something greater than human beings.

Notice that the examples from our research participants are rarely just one-word expressions. Ask yourself, "Why do I care about this?" or "What about this is important to me?"

Emma and Marcos Lopez, from Houston, Texas, illustrate the value of a deeper exploration. Emma is a management consultant and Marcos, a former captain in the army, is an investment manager. They have a four-year-old, Cole, and a seven-year-old, Megan. Emma and Marcos both listed "career success" as a core value. But this confused them because they sensed that they held quite different attitudes about their work. When we probed, it turned out career success meant something different to each of them.

Emma remembered a period of her adolescence during which her family struggled to make ends meet after her father was laid off. When she reflected on the events in her life that shaped who she is now, she realized that the intense stress her family experienced then played a significant role in forming who she became. That's why, for Emma, career success primarily means having sufficient funds stashed away and enough transferable job skills so that she does not have to worry about economic security.

For Marcos, a veteran who embraced the clear hierarchy in the military ranking system, career success meant achieving promotions and seniority. Certainly Marcos, like Emma, cares about economic security, but he does not equate it with success. Similarly, Emma cares about recognition, but it is not paramount when she thinks of what success means. To get at their core values, they had to define career success more specifically. Articulating these distinctions helped them better understand the way they each approach their careers. And when it came to thinking about what they wanted for their future, they were able to envision how they could support each other more carefully. (See the box "Identify Your Values.")

Most people assume good partners know each other's values. Yet even people who enjoy close long-term relationships are often surprised when they reveal their core values to each other. Indeed,

IDENTIFY YOUR VALUES

On your own, take thirty minutes or so to think about your values, what matters most to you and why. Come up with about five values. Write them down, perhaps take a little break, and then come back and fiddle with them, revising each one as needed. Don't limit yourself to the examples we listed. If you're still stuck, you can do an online search for a list of values and pick those that most accurately represent you. Again, you can always revise.

Many people find it helpful to reflect on significant experiences in their lives and how those episodes determined what they care about most deeply. Or, you might think of yourself not as a parent, but as a sports coach. What values would you want to impart to your players to inspire them to victory? If you identify as more history nerd than athlete, imagine you are your favorite hero and identify the essence of what you stand for. Or make up a motto. Get a bit weird if it helps you articulate your values.

Use the definition we provided as a guide: the values should be relatively stable over time and rather broad, not tied to specific people, places, and times. Take your time to find the right words, images, or stories to identify your core values—what they really mean to you and why they are important. Allow some reflection. You're likely to revise your list after thinking and talking about it. That's fine. Indeed, it's good to do so.

research has shown that we're not nearly as accurate as we think when it comes to judging the values, experiences, and goals of those closest to us.[10] You might be surprised by what you find when you share your deepest-held values.

For Emma and Marcos Lopez, discussing their values shed new light on one another, despite the fact that they've known each other for twelve years. Marcos would often get frustrated by Emma's always-on, 24/7 availability for her consulting work. He'd frequently find her lit by the glow of her laptop in bed after he assumed she was turning in for the night. It was only after learning more about Emma's family history and the traces it left that both he and Emma came to understand that her work ethic was driven, at least in part, by irrational worries about losing her economic security and a fear that she wouldn't get placed on future consulting projects if she didn't perform at a high level on the current one. When they wrote their vision together, Emma and Marcos knew it couldn't just be a pie-in-the-sky dream about pursuing their passions. For Emma to feel excited by a shared vision, it had to highlight a degree of financial security commensurate with the importance she placed on it. Later you'll see how they incorporated this element into their vision.

Describing your core values to each other and being curious about the meaning of your partner's is a crucial step in the process of finding new ways for you to parent. Your values—both those you hold in common and those that are unique to each of you—are the grist for your vision's mill. The vision will help you both live in accordance with them. (See the box "Inquire About Your Partner's Values.")

Craft a Collective Vision

We define a leadership vision as *a compelling image of an achievable future.*[11] Research has shown that creating this picture helps leaders gain a clearer sense of purpose in their careers and for their

INQUIRE ABOUT YOUR PARTNER'S VALUES

Now, relate your values to each other. You might invite your partner to read the list you created or you each might say them aloud. As you read or hear them, pay close attention. Act like a coach, gently prodding your "client" to explain why they value what they do, if it's not clear to you. But a note of caution: many of us tend to assume that people should value the same things we do, especially those with whom we've chosen to share our lives. Indeed, we've seen partners get a little freaked out when they realize their values don't entirely overlap. Avoid such judgments. Don't push your partner toward your own values. Focus instead on fully grasping theirs. While common values are important (and it's likely you'll find some), seeing differences allows you to appreciate the unique qualities you each bring to your partnership and enables you to better choose roles and responsibilities in your lives together.

While you may feel as if you've already done the important work, the best leaders take time for reflection on their experiences; this is often when the most important growth occurs.[12] Once you've discussed your values—a topic we expect you'll want to return to repeatedly—consider the following questions, and together write your responses.

1. What values do you have in common?

2. What values are unique to each one of you?

3. What did you learn about one another that you didn't already know?

organization.[13] Moreover, visions reduce stress, increase happiness in the short and long run, and drive the sustained behavioral changes needed for the vision to become real.[14] (The creation of personal vision statements is a useful tool for leader development and executive coaching. It's one of the core features of Stew's book *Total Leadership*. For more details about writing your own personal leadership vision, we refer you to chapter 2 of that book.)

There is growing recognition that effective leaders not only create their own vision for the future, but also facilitate the adoption of a shared vision, wherein team members have the *same* image of an inspiring future.[15] This allows diverse people to work together to manage the complexity of work and make decisions, alone and together, in service of this common future. A collective vision is like a lighthouse in the distance, helping us stay on our desired path and correct course when we stray.

A collective vision also acts as a beacon in personal relationships. As parents working together to navigate careers and raise children, having our own individual vision is not enough. The creation of a collective vision allows us to imagine a future we are inspired to pursue together.[16] Work/life scholar and executive coach Monique Valcour refers to a shared vision as an essential part of the "dual-career mojo that makes couples thrive."[17] Let's apply this idea to our families and to our whole lives.

Collective Visions Overcome Inertia

Parents often feel mired in their habits, even when those habits are no longer particularly useful. We're more likely to rely on our habits under conditions of time pressure and stress (conditions that are, of course, quite familiar to today's working parents).[18] But defaulting to habits often translates to resisting changes that might bring greater calm, happiness, and meaning. We succumb to a cognitive bias known in psychology as the "status quo trap" by overweighting the potential risks of changing and underestimating the potential benefits.[19] We also rely on set routines—unwavering behavioral patterns that dictate our choices and interactions with others. Reconceiving how we live can be uncomfortable, especially when we think things are good enough. So, a powerful vision that illuminates the potential for a better future helps us overcome the inertia that prevents us from making change.[20]

Rebecca and Sabrina Wayland found themselves in the status quo trap when they adopted a son fifteen months ago. Although these married women had begun the adoption process nearly two years earlier, they had only two weeks' notice between learning that they had been matched with a child and the day their newborn son, Liam, came home. Not knowing when (or if) a match would come, they hadn't spent much time working out the day-to-day logistics of dual-career parenting. The time came suddenly, and they shifted into working-parent survival mode. This mode was intensified by the fact that neither of their organizations offered benefits for adoptive parents. For Rebecca and Sabrina, survival mode meant continuing to each log seventy-plus hours of work per week—Rebecca as senior leader at a large general contractor and Sabrina as a pediatric cardiologist. To make that happen, they began waking up at 3:30 a.m. to work for three hours before Liam woke up. Because it allowed them to maintain their work status quo while caring for Liam, they considered it good enough.

Then they stepped back and looked forward, envisioning a life where they weren't in a constant state of sleep deprivation. Seeing this in writing made them wonder, "If we don't want this for our future, why are we willing to accept it for our present?" Once they asked this question, they began to look at their habits in a new way. By questioning assumptions that they were making about their time and energy, they were able to get unstuck and explore new ways of doing things.

Collective Visions Sustain Focused Energy

Compared to goals, which can get you geared up to change in the short term but can fizzle out, visions guide longer-lasting behavioral change.[21]

When you create a collective vision, you'll both be inspired to generate actionable ideas to move toward that vision and to hold each other accountable for doing so, to make the small, sustainable changes that get you on a steady path to where you want to go. You'll be committed to work toward it, not just in the days ahead, but over the years to come.

Collective Visions Get You on the Same Page

As partners, when you agree on where you're headed, you'll be better able to sort through the chaos of everyday life and work in the same direction. Organizational psychologist Andrew Carton and colleagues explain that, with an effective vision, a person can "more easily sense the collection of interdependent roles that constitute a system and understand how he or she can personally contribute" to that system.[22] For example, you'll be much more motivated to take over responsibility for doing the dishes if you understand *why* it contributes to the broader vision you share for your family (for example, it frees up your partner to care for her mental and physical fitness by taking that time to exercise). And you won't just feel resentful that another item has been added to your to-do list if you understand where it fits in the grand scheme of the values and vision you have articulated together. By creating a collective vision, you create a sense of being on the same team, moving toward a common future, rather than in competing directions or in what can feel like a haphazard hodgepodge of frenetic activity.

Collective Visions Give You a Common Language

Once you and your partner have a shared vision, you can talk about it. It can be helpful to give it a nickname (even a facetious one like "Our Path to Greatness") or put a copy of it on your fridge. Your children can see where your family is headed and get excited about being along for the ride. This is both a reminder and a source of pride. If they're old enough, they can take part in crafting the vision, too. Having a common language, or developing your own vocabulary, can help you explain your ideas to others beyond your family to inspire their support, especially if it's clear how their lives are enhanced by being a part of your journey.

Picture Tomorrow

Once Emma and Marcos Lopez identified and discussed their values, including clarifying what career success meant to each of them, they wrote a vision for their family. Here is one section of their collective vision of an ideal day, fifteen years into the future:

> It's around 6 p.m. and we just finished some cardio-heavy yoga and are getting dinner prepped together, because the kids are on their way home from college to join us for a Friday night dinner. They come home as often as possible, often bringing college friends with them for a home-cooked meal. At dinner, Megan tells us about the summer internship she has lined up to do economic development work in an underserved community somewhere in the world. Cole asks for our advice on whether he should spend the summer studying abroad or working with children locally.
>
> After the kids leave, we sit down on the couch with a glass of wine and take a moment to pat ourselves on the back for raising well-adjusted, confident children. We are glad that they do not feel pressure to make purely financially focused decisions and will not graduate with mountains of debt. They are still aware of the importance of becoming self-sufficient. They approach their studies and work with passion and vigor.
>
> We tell each other about our days. Around 9 p.m., we both pull out our laptops and answer some emails. We both still work, to stay intellectually engaged and to support our frequent adven-

tures around the world. Emma plans a lunch meeting with a colleague at her consulting firm and answers a few questions about an upcoming fundraiser for a nonprofit board. Marcos was recently made a partner at his firm, and he responds to a few questions from a new client. He also sends out a reminder about the upcoming basketball game for the team he coaches for disadvantaged Houston high school students. By 10 p.m., we're shutting down our laptops and winding down for the night. We head to bed together.

What did you notice as you read Emma and Marcos's vision? How did you feel? Did you get a little misty-eyed thinking about your own grown children coming home for an all-too-brief visit? Or did you skeptically think "Yeah, right!" when you imagined them paying for their kids' college costs and still having the money and time to travel and volunteer? Emma and Marcos were excited about it—they realized that, in some respects, they were already on the path toward making this a reality. But they also were starting to see some of the changes that they could make now to bring them closer to this vision.

We know that this vision sounds like a modern version of a fairy tale's happy ending. Of course, the future doesn't usually pan out the way that we expect.[23] "Life," as John Lennon famously sang, "is what happens to you while you're busy making other plans." If they haven't made this clear already, your children will have their own ideas about who they want to be and what they care about. Stuff happens—illness, death, an industry's collapse, untimely economic downturns—all sorts of hardships can befall us. But that doesn't diminish the power of a vision of our lives together. In fact, visions can be most useful when crises disrupt everything, by reminding us of our values and how we can hew to them or even adjust them. So, go ahead and imagine the possibilities. (See the box "Describe Your Ideal Day.")

It's not always a frictionless process for partners to create a vision. If you're struggling through the exercise of creating a collective vision,

DESCRIBE YOUR IDEAL DAY

Draft your own collective vision. Write the story of what happens in a single day in your lives fifteen years from today. Try to include these pieces:

- What you do in the morning, in the afternoon, and in the evening

- How you feel about what you're doing

- How you relate to one another, your children, and other important people

- What your children are like and what they're doing on this day

- Why you are doing what you're doing

you're not alone. Based on our experiences working with partnerships in the past, here are some questions to ask yourselves that may help you troubleshoot visions that aren't quite working for you.

Are Our Commonly Held and Unique Values Both Represented?

Your collective vision should emphasize the values you have in common while also providing room for each of you to pursue the particular values that distinguish you. Emma and Marcos had little difficulty incorporating their shared values, like volunteerism and intellectual curiosity, into their vision. They had to work a little harder to ensure that Emma's need for financial security and Marcos's love of competition were both represented, as well.

Consider whether your vision empowers you to embody both your shared *and* unique values. It's easy to focus on how your vision will represent your shared values and to ignore the rest, perhaps hoping that conflicts will just resolve themselves. They usually don't. Are any essential values missing? By putting the time in now to figure out a way for your values to coexist in the future, you are investing in the likely prospect of a smoother ride.

Does It Address All Domains of Our Lives?

For most of us, our home lives aren't our whole lives. Consider your careers and your communities, as well as your own well-being and growth. Notice how Emma and Marcos described not just the family life they aspire to, but also their careers, community work, and care for themselves. How is what you are doing on that imagined day representing the values you hold for the kind of people you want to be as parents *and* in the impact you yearn to make through your work, your role in the larger world, and the way you live your lives?

Can We Actually Envision It?

While it may be tempting to write a broad, generic vision (for example, "We will be happy and healthy"), these sorts of statements don't ignite the imagination or inspire commitment in the same way that vividly descriptive visions do.[24] Moreover, general visions don't push you to talk through what you want your lives to be. By drafting a specific vision, you make it more likely that you're both on the same page moving forward. Your vision needs to be vivid enough so you both can see it clearly and feel this picture's emotional pull.

Does It Strongly Appeal to Both of Us?

This experience should be fun (for the most part). By writing a vision statement you both love, the rest of our advice in this book will feel a lot more like an adventure than a chore. After composing their collective vision, Emma and Marcos were fired up to start moving toward it. While they found the process to be a positive experience that flowed easily for them, that isn't always the case. If this vision became a reality, would you feel proud and content with the life you created?

Do We Want the Same Things?

A major sticking point for many parenting partnerships is that their visions of the future aren't the same. We worked with a couple where one partner aspired to a career of serial entrepreneurship, while the other longed for more stability and routine. This fundamental disagreement threatened to derail them from working as a parenting team. We encouraged them to first develop a better understanding of what exactly they each wanted from their lives. Simply expressing their desired futures allowed them to engage in dialogue that brought them closer together. It began a longer conversation about how they might build toward a future that met each of their respective needs and created hope where there had previously been frustration. There may not be a quick fix to deep-seated differences in what you want your lives to look like. But it's important to get that conversation started now, so that you can make conscious choices together about the path that you will take.

Does Our Vision Seem Possible?

Another stumbling block emerges when a vision seems impossibly far from the life you're living right now, with no clear path to get there. One of the parenting partnerships in our research, Brian and Tyler Wang-Novak, dreamed of travel and adventure as a family, free from the demands of traditional nine-to-five office jobs. But this vision seemed so unrealistic that they almost didn't want to write it down. But they did. And once they did, they asked themselves, Why not now? This simple question sparked a series of conversations that led them to making profound changes in their lifestyle. Within six months of creating their vision, they had already rented out their home and lived in three different countries. They experienced satisfaction and personal growth, particularly as they witnessed the meaningful impact this adventure was having on their children.

Starting with an impossible dream can reveal a lot of useful information about what you want your lives to look like today. We've all heard the saying, "It's not the destination, it's the journey." Moving toward your vision is a long-term endeavor in which you're striving to enact your values. A primary purpose of articulating your shared vision is not just to get you to some desirable end state but to help you see more clearly what it might mean to live your life in way that's better aligned with your values *now*. You might realize that what you want in the future is within your reach now.

So, allow yourself to dream big, knowing that if you work toward that vision but don't get 100 percent of the way there, there's still much to be gained by expressing a compelling direction you want your lives to take. If the benefits are not yet obvious to you, we are certain they will become evident as we progress through the chapters that follow.

Is Our Vision Boring?

Some parenting partnerships face the opposite problem. They're so bogged down in the day-to-day that they can't even envision a life outside their current groove. That's what happened to Winston and Mia Li. A dynamic Silicon Valley couple with two young boys, Winston and Mia are extroverts whom you can't help but notice, especially because Winston always wears his hair styled in a three-inch pompadour. Compared to their engaging personalities, their collective vision felt like a snooze. It looked almost exactly like a day in their current life, albeit with older kids, slightly more senior positions at work, and a bit more relaxation. This vision left them uninspired and rather depressed.

When they dug deeper, they realized they didn't even consider options that were fundamentally different from their lives now. We encouraged them to go old-school and start with a vision board of magazine images representing their desired future. They opted to pin images to an online board instead. Because they felt freer to use their imagination, a different picture emerged—one removed from big-city living, out of the Silicon Valley rat race, immersed in nature, and closer to extended family. Enthusiasm ensued.

Like Winston and Mia, we encourage you to take the time to imagine what you really want. You can get out your glue stick and try the vision board idea. Or, you can visualize yourselves as children again, thinking about what you want your lives to be like when you grow up. Or, picture yourselves receiving a lifetime achievement award and listening to the description of your accomplishments. (A more morbid version of this would be to write your eulogy.) Find whatever creative method suits you and then see what you discover and what pathways start to open.

And keep this in mind: you can always revise.

Chapter 3

EMBRACE THE
FOUR-WAY VIEW

Most of us, whether we realize it or not, tend to adopt a trade-off mind-set in thinking about the different facets of our lives. We assume we're playing a zero-sum game.[1] In other words, we see the different aspects of our lives as a fixed pie, with our time and attention divided into set slices, and we believe gains in one area of life, whether it be in our work or in our family relationships, automatically come with losses to the other areas.[2] The desire for a larger slice here means a smaller slice there.

While we don't deny that trade-offs exist, our research has shown that it's fruitful to adopt a more expansive attitude, in which trade-offs are not the default assumption. Instead, we can seek opportunities to create wins as leaders in *all* the roles we play. The possibility of such wins *is* there, but we have to look for them if we're going to be able to pursue them and produce harmonious flow.

We're now going to address crucial aspects of producing a stronger, more trusting parenting partnership. When you are honest about where you each are right now, in all parts of your lives, you are in a much stronger position to move forward collaboratively. In later chapters, we'll move outward to help you understand others who are your life-blood, starting with your children. Your growth will be more successful if you do this careful, candid mapping of who matters most. But first, the partnership.

Sabra and Aryan Kabir are Israeli expats who've been living in Hartford, Connecticut, for the past eleven years. Their daughter Danya is nine and their son Adar is four. Three years ago, Aryan founded a medical supply company and Sabra went back to work part-time as a freelance consultant in the insurance industry. When we met them, they both agreed things were "OK." They were able to keep up with the stuff of everyday life to get their work done and care for Danya and Adar. But they had little time for anything else and felt they were just going through the motions. They were frustrated because they sensed they were missing out—not enough joy, too little fulfillment.

They came to our workshop because they were searching for something more. When they created their collective vision, the idea of what "more" looked like began to crystallize. They imagined themselves back in Israel near their extended family, raising their children in a culture they loved and creating their own environmental conservation business. They were exuberant about this vision, but how to progress from their present circumstances to that dream was a complete mystery. What choices would move them through the days, weeks, months, and years toward their vision? We encouraged Sabra and Aryan to take a new perspective on their lives today. Once they were able to see the bigger picture of their whole lives right now—on their own and together—they were able to make changes that brought them nearer to their dreamed-of future and to find greater purpose in the present.

First, they came to realize that they had adopted a divide-and-conquer approach, and it wasn't working for them. Sabra took care of the children's emotional needs, providing comfort and affection. Aryan managed all the finances. He spent long hours at the office working on the business he had created. Sabra worked only when she could squeeze it in around the family schedule. They recognized that the long, stressful hours Aryan was putting into his startup left him drained, not able to focus on Sabra and their children when he was with them. So, Sabra compensated by concentrating more on the children. She wanted to shield them from Aryan's short fuse and protect Aryan from additional stress after he got home. But this left him feeling disconnected from his family, like a bystander.

They also saw that their communication centered mainly on logistics. To an outsider, it looked as though they operated like a well-oiled machine. But on the inside, it was a different story. Their sense of meaning was vacant, and their relationships with each other and with friends were thin. They longed for a common spirit, for fun, and for a deeper appreciation of the good things in life.

These insights spurred innovations to reinvigorate their passion for one another and the simple pleasures of their life. They instituted weekly meetings to cover all logistics in one fell swoop (for example, pickups and drop-offs, late workdays, family mealtimes). They started family game nights, playing everything from *Settlers of Catan* to *Scrabble*, to help them rediscover the lightness of being with each other. This improved Aryan's capacity to be psychologically present— not just physically present—when he was in the same room with his loved ones. This, in turn, reduced his stress level *and* his orneriness with colleagues.

In later chapters, we'll guide you in developing your ideas for making things better for both of you and for others. But smart innovations don't usually present themselves as random bolts out of the blue. Sabra and Aryan developed theirs by starting with their collective vision and then undertaking a process of taking the four-way view.

Let's look first at your life as a whole and then get a better feel for how you and your partner influence each other. As you examine the status quo, ideas for constructive change will start to pop up, and you'll want to keep track of them. In the meantime, be prepared to join forces in learning more about what your children need and to build support in your world for the vision you're pursuing together.

As we proceed, do whatever you can to remain open to challenging your assumptions so that you can clarify what you really need and uncover the important ways your lives touch each other. Emulate the finest leaders, who remain genuinely curious, continually seeking new knowledge as they look for opportunities to make life better for others.[3]

Examine the Four Domains

For simplicity's sake, we focus on four major arenas of life, what we refer to as the four domains: career, family, community, and self. As we describe each one, consider what the domain means to you, how you would characterize it, and how it relates to the others. Challenging the trade-off mindset starts with digging deep to reveal each part. In later chapters, we'll dig further still.

Career

Jobs are what we do to make money. But careers are more than that. We have careers that extend throughout our lives, starting and stopping, growing and changing.[4] For some people, work is only a way to make the money they need to live. While work doesn't *have* to be an expression of our deeper purpose, life is better for most people when it is.[5] Most working parents spend the majority of their waking hours in professional pursuits.[6] So, it's good to think of our careers as an ongoing aspect of our lives that unfolds over time. And if you're not in paid employment at this moment, it doesn't mean you are without a career. You may choose to go back into the paid workforce part-time or full-time, or you may double-down on homemaking or volunteer work and allow it to become your true calling.[7] The career domain can include education, too, whether you're in school now or considering going back.

People are as important as the work itself in defining a four-way view. Who are the people most important to your career, especially in light of your values and vision? They may be collaborators in your volunteer work or colleagues or clients in your current job. The people who loom large today may not be the most important figures in the broader span of your career, especially as you look to the future, so consider your wider-reaching professional network. Focus on who has shaped your trajectory or who might do so. This could include former coworkers, mentors, professors, or anyone else important for your growth. Of course, your career might change. But, for now, take a mental snapshot of the constellation of people who matter in this domain.

Family

This domain encompasses our lives as children, parents, and partners. It can include extended family, too, distant cousins, in-laws, and out-laws.

Like everything else we ask you to ponder, it is entirely up to you to decide the meaning of family. It may be that the people you define as family are not genetically or legally related to you. The popular comedian Greg Fitzsimmons and his wife, Erin, adopted the term "framily" to describe those friends they consider to be part of their family. A portmanteau of friends and family, framily gives Greg and Erin the freedom to define family on their own terms, signaling a degree of love and trust that extends deeper than the common conceptualization of friendship. Perhaps your family includes animals (there's a reason people call pets "fur babies"). You may have cherished elders you call "Aunty" and "Uncle," or you may have a family that you lived with as an exchange student. You may have "stepchildren" from former lovers. Don't just consider individual people as you think about your clan. It might even be another family that you spend every Thanksgiving with. Consider the different roles you play in this extended family.

Family might be envisioned as concentric rings of a tree, with you and your nuclear family at the center. Or it might also be thought of as a wheel with a hub and spokes or a constellation linking many small groups of stars. Everyone has a unique understanding of what's meant by family—our most intimate and often our most challenging relationships.

Community

This part is usually the hardest for parents, especially those with young children, to wrap their minds around. When we ask workshop participants to define "community," we often hear something like "I'm too busy with work and family to have any time for community." Still, it's fruitful to consider this aspect of life. Include in this stream anything that's about life beyond career and family. Think about the village that helps you raise your children—teachers, godparents, childcare providers, sports coaches, scout troop leaders, neighbors, friends, the parents of your children's friends. As we get further into your exploration of community, you might come to see some of these people as integral parts of the support system you need to thrive.

Consider your network of friends and relationships that exist beyond your role as parents; members of religious or social groups, for example, or fellow gym rats, running partners, or members of Toastmasters or your college alumni network. Community can also involve political or charitable affiliations. For Marcos, the former army captain, his community included fellow members of the Wounded Warrior Project, an organization that supports veterans harmed in military combat, of which he is one. Even if you don't have such affiliations now, as we'll explain later, it's helpful to think about bridges to the world beyond your family and work.

Self

This too-often overlooked domain comprises your body, mind, and spirit. This is not outward facing—toward others—but rather inward facing. It includes your physical and mental health, your spiritual pursuits, and relaxation. Find ways to identify facets of who you are and the things you do to cultivate yourself as an individual.

PHYSICAL HEALTH. Physical health includes sleep, nutrition, and exercise. But it also includes other ways by which we care (or don't care) for our bodies. Elements of this domain might include everything from getting massages to flossing our teeth.

What do you need to thrive physically? We try to avoid preaching, but we'll make an exception here. To be healthy, experts have found the average person needs seven hours of sleep per night.[8] If you think you can run on consistently less sleep than that without experiencing any negative effects, you're probably wrong. Sleep-deprived people are generally unable to estimate the toll that chronic lack of rest takes on them.[9] Sleep is one key element in the self domain.

What else does your body need? One of our workshop participants pointed out that she needs "routine visits to the doctor and dentist and age-appropriate health screenings." Seems like common sense, but we know how easy it can be to let these things fall by the wayside.

MENTAL HEALTH. Mental health refers to the psyche, our inner lives, our emotional well-being. For some of us, this includes issues that dampen well-being, such as anxiety and depression. Managing stress, regulating emotions, learning how to cope with our frailties, generating positive feelings, and maintaining relationships that enrich our lives are all aspects of this domain.

Like physical health, caring for mental health comes in an almost infinite variety of forms. It might mean simply a weekly phone date with a good friend to touch base, vent, or share highs and lows. By whatever means you go about it, managing stress is an essential feature of taking care of yourself. For some, taking care of mental health might mean regular therapy sessions to manage social anxiety, an addiction, or any number of conditions. Getting professional help can be the difference between life and death. Seeking a diagnosis, finding a therapist, or getting on the right medication can not only improve your own wellness, but also allow you to better support your partner, your children, your colleagues, and your world.

SPIRITUALITY. The pursuit of spiritual satisfaction varies from person to person. For some, it may involve organized religion, whereas for others, it might be belonging to a Zen community or participating in a spiritual retreat. It could be as low-key as a meditation app, a gratitude journal, or walks in nature.

Consider what, if anything, you need to feel fulfilled in your spiritual growth. Workshop participant Luke Bailey, a chief technology officer and "hockey dad" of two young boys, found spiritual fulfillment through organized religion. He wrote, "I want to be the spiritual leader of my family. I should have time praying, reading the Bible, and reflecting on a daily basis." Many people find nonreligious paths to connect to something bigger than themselves. What you need to feel fulfilled spiritually is unique to you; reading this book may help you define or refine your sense of spirituality.

RELAXATION. Relaxation has physical, mental, and spiritual dimensions—it's about finding time to recharge your batteries in whatever way works best for you. Whether it's taking regular vacations, getting a facial, watching a film, reading for pleasure, or going for a walk, relaxation time is another element of what we refer to as your self domain.

An important aspect of your own private world is the time you take to just shut it down, rather than constantly completing your list of things that must be done.[10] We often hear from people that they're just "not good at relaxing" or that they've actually even forgotten what they like to do to relax. Researchers have documented the beneficial effects of recovery at the end of a workday; it can buffer us from the aches that come from too much work. It can reduce fatigue, boost energy, and enhance general well-being.[11] Moreover, it improves concentration at work the subsequent day.[12] It's no wonder that *niksen*, the Dutch word for the practice of doing nothing, is gaining popularity as a remedy to burnout and stress.[13] Consider what a break from your own task list looks like; of course, it's not going be the same as what other people do to unwind. For some, going for a run might be a delightful form of relaxation; for others, this is yet another thing on their already too-long list.[14] For others, a glass of wine while savoring the sunset does the trick, while for others still, laughing with their children is what's needed to recharge.

Notice How the Strands Weave

Taking the four-way view means seeing how these domains of life are interconnected. Of course, different areas of our lives come with obligations that can disturb others. As but one obvious example, working long, high-stress hours can have a negative impact on all other areas of life.[15] If you've ever been snippy at the dinner table after a tough day at the office, you know what we mean. Similarly, challenges in our family lives don't just magically disappear at work.[16] People caring for sick children, assisting aging parents, or going through divorce tend to be less productive. Our physical and mental well-being profoundly influences both our work and our private experiences.

Researchers have spent a lot of effort studying various forms of conflict between work and the rest of life, how they disrupt each other. But we like to flip the frame: career, family, community, and self can also be mutually enriching.[17] It's not always easy or natural to steer clear of the zero-sum mentality, captured in the phrase almost everyone uses to describe the challenge of finding harmony—"work/life balance." But it's important to counter our tendency to think in terms of a metaphor of that sliced-up pie where more of one slice means less of another.

There are countless examples that demonstrate the power of envisioning the possibilities for harmony, or four-way wins. It's obvious that work provides financial resources that are used to support our families.[18] But beyond that, our careers can give us opportunities to express our values, benefit others, build relationships, and establish our identities. Work can be a refuge, too, a source of renewal. You've probably had moments when you breathed a sigh of relief as you sat down at a quiet desk to work after scrambling to meet the incessant demands of young children.

Similarly, our family lives can give us the inspiration to be successful at work.[19] Our partners can be sounding boards for career advice.[20] The various people in our families can give us insight if we are artists, ideas if we are inventors, stories we can tell to bond with colleagues, and so much more.[21]

Along the same lines, our communities can help us raise our children, lead to job opportunities, and inspire us to express our values.[22] Taking care of our physical and mental states can give us the strength to meet challenges, the focus to perform well at work, and the gratitude to appreciate our children and our communities.[23]

Each facet of our lives informs and influences the others. The four-way view allows us to not just *see* the many dimensions of our lives, but also enables us to cultivate harmony. Here's what some of the parents we've worked with observed when they examined the interconnections among the different aspects of their lives:

> Satisfaction in one area affects my mood and general happiness and thus allows me to perform well in the other areas of my life.

> When I work out and take time for myself, I am more likely to respond to my kids with kindness and grace.

> When I am particularly happy with family life, or on a really good stretch of running, I tend to take that attitude to work and feel good about myself, and more confident. But I also often find myself letting the opposite happen. When things are particularly stressful at work, sometimes I can be short-tempered and less patient with my family.

TAKE THE FOUR-WAY VIEW

What do the different parts of your life mean to you? Spend some time brainstorming about each of the four domains—career, family, community, and self. Think about what you do, with whom you interact, what you need, and what you care about most in each of those domains. Write down ideas, phrases, and names that come to mind. Or try drawing pictures of yourself at work, at home, in your community, and taking care of yourself (you don't need talent as an artist to do so—stick figures are fine).

Once you have a good sense of how you define each domain, complete the table as best you can. Recognize that you and your partner—and anyone else—might define the domains in a different way, and that's perfectly all right. Complete the table about yourself, not your partner or the two of you together.

My four-way view

Domain	Importance	Attention	Satisfaction (1–10)
Career	%	%	
Family	%	%	
Community	%	%	
Self	%	%	
	100%	100%	

The second column asks you how important each of the four domains is to you. These numbers should add up to 100 percent. If all four parts are of equal importance to you, then it's 25, 25, 25, and 25. If family is the only thing that matters, then it's 0, 100, 0, and 0. Play around with these numbers until they seem right.

(continued)

Next, think about how much attention you actually focus on each domain in a typical week or a typical month. Focus doesn't just mean how much time you spend in a particular location. It's about where your mind is (during your waking hours). You might, for example, be sitting at the dining table with your family while you are obsessively revisiting an unfortunate episode you had with a client earlier in the day. Your attention, in this instance, is on work, even as you're sitting next to your child. Assign a percentage to each domain to represent the portion of your attention you devote to each domain and be sure that these numbers also add up to another 100 percent.

Finally, in the last column, rate how satisfied you are with each domain on a scale of 1 to 10, with 1 meaning "not at all satisfied" and 10 meaning "fully satisfied." If you are brimming with a sense of fellowship because of the fullness of your church life, give community a 9 or a 10. If you never find time to take care of your physical health or to relax, this would push your self score down the scale. This is your subjective sense of how things are going for you in this area of your life—as you see it, how you feel about it, not how others would assess this from their vantage point.

Once you've filled out the table, reflect on what it tells you. Notice the interconnections. Think about how the attention you dedicate to one domain affects the others, positively or negatively.

By the time you're done with this book, you'll have a new appreciation of the possibilities for four-way wins in your lives—individually and together. Let's next explore how you can become more skilled in the ability to find harmony among the domains of your life. (See the box "Take the Four-Way View.")

Consider where there may be gaps between what is most impor-tant to you and how you actually allocate your attention. Observe how satisfaction in one part influences how things are going in the others.

What ideas occur to you about how changing something in one part might lead to improvements in how things go in other parts? If you were to spend one day a week telecommuting, for instance, how might this affect your engagement with your family, community, and private self? If you were to take your family to the beach rather than going alone to the gym, how would the satisfaction levels with your family and self domains shift?

After you've completed your work with the table, find a journal or sketchbook and write your responses to these questions:

1. How are the different numbers in your table connected to each other?

2. What patterns do you see that tell you what's working well and what's not?

3. What's the biggest obstacle you would face, *besides time*, in trying to change things to increase overall satisfaction and gen-erate a greater feeling of harmony?

You might find it helpful to know you're not alone if you rate your satisfaction as less than 10 across the board in your four-way view. Among the parents in our workshops, not a single person has yet rated their satisfaction with career or family as a 10 out of 10. There were plenty of 1's and 2's, though. Across the four domains, average levels of satisfaction tend to hover around a 5 out of 10. While it might not change your sense of well-being, knowing that others—almost everyone, really—are wrestling with these challenges will likely help you feel normal. Life is hard these days, for all of us. But, remember, when you start out not fully satisfied, this allows room for growth. That's just math.

Overcome Inhibitions to Creative Thinking

The reason that we ask you to consider obstacles *other than* a lack of time when evaluating your four-way view is that people get so hung up saying "If I just had more time . . . ," they fail to see the other ways in which their thought process might be blocking opportunities for change. Let's look a little more closely at these common self-limiting beliefs so that you can see if any apply to you and how you think about the different domains.

Perfectionism

The first thing many people do when they look at their four-way view is to criticize themselves. Parents often look at their numbers and infer they should be less lazy, inefficient, impatient, and disorganized. They blame themselves for anything less than 10s down the right column. Try not to let perfectionism rear its ugly head. It can destroy the capacity for discovery, especially for overachievers who've benefited from the drive that perfectionism has instilled in them.[24] Perfectionistic thinking has you just putting your head down and working harder, believing that if you do so, you should be able to make everything right. Perfectionistic thinking prevents you from letting go and seeing how a new project goes, and then making adjustments later. Loosen your grip on the idea that the only thing standing between you and perfection is your willpower.

It's normal to struggle with the four-way view when the numbers seem somehow awry. For parents who participated in our workshops, on average, their careers took up 57 percent of their attention—far greater than the importance they placed on them, which averaged 33 percent. The opposite trend held for family, which got an average of a 34 percent importance rating but only 25 percent of attention. Community was often seen as less important (12 percent), but parents were dedicating even less (only 6 percent) of their attention to cultivating those relationships. Finally, even though parents viewed taking care of themselves as moderately important (20 percent), they were devoting just about half that amount of attention to the self domain (around 11 percent). Misalignment is inevitable at this stage. Try to calm the part of your mind that prods you to think that your table *should* somehow look better. In other words, be compassionate with yourself.

Guilt

If you're like most people reading this book, you feel guilty admitting dissatisfaction. In a time when the world can seem bleak, when so many people have life-and-death struggles, your own attempts to find harmony between work and the rest of life might make you feel guilty about not being fully satisfied. In recent conversations with friends, one of us (Alyssa) has heard more than one of them say, "How can I complain about being too busy when there are children at the border being kept in cages away from their parents?" But knowing that others have it worse does not diminish our own sense of imbalance. It's possible to recognize how fortunate we are and still want things to be better—for ourselves *and* for others.

So, if you're feeling such guilt, remember that striving to increase satisfaction isn't wrong or greedy. There is a reason people on airplanes are advised to put on their own oxygen masks before helping others. Your role as a parent raising the next generation is important. Taking care of yourself and living your values allows you to be a role model for your children and help them thrive. Beyond your own children, you may be in a position to make real changes in our world that might make things better for others. But you can't help others if you're running on empty. So, think about the impact you might like to have on others, and instead of letting your guilt stop you, try to reframe your actions. You want to give to your family, and you want to contribute to the world. That's what leaders do.

Fear of Change

When we take a hard look at ourselves, it's not surprising that we worry about all the downsides to potential change. We fail to think creatively about the potential for new and better ways of doing things. Earlier, we described how a leadership vision can serve to overcome the inertia caused by the bias people have in favor of the status quo. Some psychologists blame this inhibition on "loss aversion tendencies."[25] This is the fear that if we enact change, our circumstances might worsen; this tends to outweigh our optimism that things could get better.[26] And so we settle for the "devil we know," that is, the status quo. It leads to a very real difficulty in letting go of habits, of fixed ideas about what works, or of the way we've come to identify ourselves. Anxiety can start to pop up when we take a systematic look at what matters and what we focus our minds on. Try not to worry too much, yet, about the awful things that might transpire if you actually tried to implement new ideas.

All-or-Nothing Thinking

Another common trap we fall into when drawing conclusions about ourselves is all-or-nothing thinking.[27] One workshop participant said that in order "to feel good about my parenting, I would need to quit my job and be completely focused on my kids. I can't do that, so that means I am always going to be dissatisfied." Her all-or-nothing thinking—"The only way to be satisfied in my family life would be to quit my job"—tends to inhibit creativity and prevents experimenting with new perspectives and potential solutions.

As you interpret your own four-way view table, be on the lookout for black-and-white thinking. Ask yourself whether a middle ground is possible. You don't have to know what it is just yet. For instance, you could ask yourself, "Is it *possible* that there's a way to have a job and be satisfied with my family life?" Acknowledging the possibility of another way is a crucial step to challenging this sort of crippling black-and-white thought process.

Explore Both of Your Four-Way Views

Now that you have a more complete picture of where you are and have started to think anew about the connections among your different domains and the whole person they are all part of—you—it's time to explore interconnections between your life and your partner's, from the point of view of the four domains. They are always intertwined, whether or not we take the time to notice those interconnections.[28] To move intelligently and compassionately toward your collective vision, you need to understand how the different areas of your life shape your partner's, and vice versa. How, for example, does your career affect your partner's experience as a parent? How do your partner's spiritual pursuits affect your ability to stay connected with your friends and community?

Research shows that moods and emotions are contagious between partners, much like the common cold. If one comes home stressed, angry, or frustrated, the other experiences stress, too. The time and energy your partner spends at work, with your children, in the community, and on their health can either wreck or renew you.[29] Research shows that when one partner has a rough day at work, they are more likely to act angrily, be short-tempered, or withdraw at home, on top of being more likely to stay late at work. Work stress results in yet more demands at home and less emotional support for the other partner, making it harder for the other to manage work and causing greater exhaustion.[30]

Joy and enthusiasm, happily, are also contagious. One study found that on days when one partner was more positively engaged at work, the other partner experienced significantly greater happiness.[31] On days when we feel supported by our work colleagues, we are more generous and supportive at home.[32] Emotions and experiences at work, both good and bad, pass between partners every day.

Regardless of how close you are to your partner, they have a private, complex inner life to which you are not always privy. Yet, generally speaking, the more you know about each other, the easier it is to forge your lives together. When your partner shares their perceptions about you in the different domains of your life, two wonderful things can happen. First, you gain greater self-awareness by seeing yourself through another's eyes. You might not recognize the messages you're sending until you actually hear the other point of view. Second, you have the opportunity to correct some assumptions that your partner may be making about you. And, conversely, when you reveal how you perceive your partner in the fullness of their various roles, the reverse benefits emerge. Through these exchanges, you gain a greater understanding of how your lives flow together and how you can provide the loving support that will make your partnership fruitful and fun. (See the box "Assess Your Partner's Four-Way View and What You Need from Each Other.")

I (Stew) and my wife, Hallie, went to visit our eldest son when he was living in Manaus, a city in northwestern Brazil accessible only by air or water. On our first day, his friends took us to the river. There, the Amazon is actually two rivers—the dark Rio Negro and the pale Rio Solimões—flowing together side by side. We could see clearly they were different; connected yet separate, two bodies of water right next to each other, as one. We talked about how our partnership is like the Amazon as it rolls through Manaus, with its pink river dolphins and its warm, welcoming inhabitants. To this day, we still refer to our partnership as a meeting of the waters.

ASSESS YOUR PARTNER'S FOUR-WAY VIEW AND WHAT YOU NEED FROM EACH OTHER

Complete the four-way view table, again. But this time, complete it about each other. Don't fuss about your accuracy: you're simply providing your best, subjective estimate about your partner. How important do you believe your partner feels each of the domains are? From your perspective, how much attention does your partner pay to each? How satisfied do you think your partner is (from 1 to 10, with 1 meaning "not at all satisfied" and 10, "fully satisfied")?

My partner's four-way view

Domain	Importance	Attention	Satisfaction (1–10)
Career	%	%	
Family	%	%	
Community	%	%	
Self	%	%	
	100%	100%	

Now, take a few minutes on your own and write about the following questions:

1. What did you notice about the interconnections among the different domains within your partner's life? How does importance, attention, or satisfaction in one part either nourish or starve the others?

2. Consider each of the four parts of your partner's life. How are *you* affected by the importance, attention, and satisfaction in each of your partner's domains?

(continued)

When you're done with this table and the two questions about it, spend some time contemplating what you really need from your partner and the extent to which your partner is meeting those needs. Write down some notes about what you need from your partner. Then, using the simple scale of 1 (poorly) to 10 (fully), consider how well they are doing in meeting those needs. It might seem awkward, but try it, and get ready to hear your partner's subjective truth when you share your perceptions with each other. If it's helpful, find another method of evoking this information, perhaps through a collage of images that conveys your experience. Just get it out there, by whatever means works for you.

Then flip. Try to understand what your partner needs from you and how well you're meeting those needs, on that same scale of 1 to 10. After some reflection, write notes to capture your insights:

1. What do you really need from your partner? And how well is your partner doing in meeting these needs (1 to 10)?

2. What does your partner really need from you? And how well are you doing in meeting your partner's needs (1 to 10)?

Invite your partner to read what you wrote about their four-way view and your assessment of each other's needs and how well they're being met. Or share it all aloud together. It's important to explain *why* you responded in the way that you did. This can get tricky—you may raise some hackles if you are perceived as criticizing how, for instance, your partner prioritizes attention. Proceed with compassion. Enter this exchange in a spirit of inquiry. You're not seeking revenge here. Rather, you're striving to face reality and looking to your shared future, expressing genuine interest in walking common ground.

Take the Leadership Leap

You might think you know each other's interests entirely. But we're willing to bet you don't, because we hear about such surprises all the time. Yet you need to know. To more completely share responsibility for your children and your lives together, it helps to continually improve your ability to grasp your partner's perspective. Indeed, doing so makes it all possible. Yet for most of us, taking the "leadership leap"—seeing ourselves through the eyes of those around us—is not a natural act.[33] It's hard to transcend natural self-centeredness, but with practice we can build stronger empathy muscles.[34] The rest of this chapter offers further guidelines on how to make the most of the opportunity to build trust in your partnership through dialogue about each other's four-way views and about how you can provide mutual support.

Share Your Four-Way Views

As you talk with your partner about what you see when you look at each other's lives from the perspective of all four domains, it's useful to reflect on how the complexities of your partner's life affect you and your lives together. Do so with the impression of your collective vision in mind. How, in other words, does your partner's current four-way view match up with that desired future?

Lily Conrad is married to Brad Conrad, who is a web designer and old-car enthusiast, and they have a three-year-old daughter, Zainah. When Lily and Brad took a step back to discuss how they perceived one another's four-way views and how they influenced each other, some of their beliefs about each other were reaffirmed. But, also, new light was shed on things they hadn't noticed before. For example, Brad thought Lily was dedicating about 40 percent of her time to their family, whereas Lily saw it as 70 percent. While there's no easy, clear way to get a reading on how much attention Lily gives to family (after all, we're talking about where her mind is, not simply where she is physically), it sparked an important conversation about how much time Lily spends doing family-related tasks while at her project management job, like scheduling doctors' appointments or making a quick Target run during her lunch break.

Brad realized that Lily's compulsion to get work done after Zainah went to bed wasn't just about the importance she placed on work as a project manager; it was also about her feeling that she didn't have enough opportunity during the day to get everything done. This conversation allowed Brad to see Lily's late-night work sessions in a more realistic light, and it led to a negotiation about when and how those family-related tasks could be accomplished with greater awareness of their needs at work and in other parts of their lives.

Lily realized she actually wanted to participate in more community activities with Brad. This was just one piece of the picture that became clearer when they shared their four-way views. Brad, the more social of the pair, felt he had to force Lily into hanging out with other families or going on adventures in their neighborhood. She never seemed that excited about his plans for a Formula 1 race-viewing party or a walk to the newest microbrewery in town. Until they had this conversation, he didn't realize how much she appreciated that he acted as "social chairperson" in their relationship. While Lily acknowledged that she rarely initiated those plans, she didn't want Brad to feel guilty about forcing her into these activities. To the contrary, this conversation prompted them to brainstorm about how they could do even more to connect with their neighbors and how that would strengthen their own relationship and Zainah's feeling of belonging to a larger world.[35]

Understand Each Other's Needs

Talking about what you really seek from your partner might seem daunting, so before you start, let's see how one couple approached the

challenge. We asked Peter and Camila Orlov, Los Angeles–based food-
ies with a young daughter and another one on the way, to write about
what they turn to each other for. We also asked them to rate, on a scale
of 1 to 10, how well the other partner is doing in meeting those needs.
We then asked them to reverse and write what they think their partner
wants from them.

Peter, an investment banker, told us that among other things, he
wants Camila, a retail industry executive, "to be a daily participant in
the domestic responsibilities of running a household. I want her, just
like she wants me, to be an active participant in our daughter's intellectual and physical development." All in all, he rated her highly: "She
is an 8 out of 10 in meeting these needs," he said. Putting himself in
Camila's shoes, one point he made was that "Camila expects me to take
care of myself and my physical and emotional health, which I arguably
do poorly." Overall, he said, "I believe I'm meeting her needs about a
4 out of 10."

Camila shared her perspective on their mutual expectations alongside corresponding numerical ratings. Camila said, "I need him to recognize that being a working mom is extremely challenging, especially
with my tough career. I wish I could spend more time at home, and I
need forgiveness from him because I don't." She added that, right now,
"Peter is about a 5 out of 10." About Peter's expectations of her, she
said that he "really wants to feel like I'm in his corner. This sometimes
means respecting his decision even if I don't agree with it (like when
we should take away our daughter's pacifier)." She rated herself as a
7 out of 10 in meeting his needs.

Peter and Camila Orlov saw the fabric of their interwoven lives and
began to articulate what they really want to ask of one another as they
move into the future together. This was the first time they discussed
how much Camila desires affirmation from Peter. Peter was dumb-
founded when he learned that Camila felt the need for forgiveness. He
assumed Camila knew it was obvious that she was doing an amazing

job as a working mother, so he never bothered to say it out loud. Hearing this from Peter, at long last, took a huge weight off her shoulders and even changed how she saw herself. And Camila reinforced Peter's supposition that she worries about him not taking sufficient care of his health, something she had avoided saying in the past for fear of putting undue pressure on him.

There is much to be gained in this conversation. Keep in mind these guidelines for engaging in it in a productive way:[36]

- Treat your perceptions as limited to what you know, not objective facts. You might say something like this: "Here's how I see it, but I know I'm not seeing the whole picture, so what am I missing?"

- Ask for details and examples to clarify meaning and increase understanding. This is especially important if you are truly confused—perhaps shocked—by what you read or hear.

- Try, try, and try again to avoid being defensive or blaming your partner. Do your best to remain open and inquiring. Understand how your partner sees you as well as you possibly can.

- Focus on building your shared future together and not on rehashing the past. Try to see the past as a springboard to propel you forward to where you want to go. Remember the value of optimism.

- Don't worry about making agreements to change things, yet. The main purpose here is to deepen understanding and trust. Keep notes of good ideas for changes that might emerge but avoid drilling down into them just yet. Keep in mind that the more long-lasting changes in how you lead together tend to come from a thoughtful consideration of not just what you need from each other, but how these interests play out in the larger context. We'll get there.

We've all got baggage, and it's not hard to enumerate all the ways your partner has wronged you. Everyone's got a list. The line between *cruel* and *honest* can get blurry. Say what needs to be said; talking about things heretofore left unsaid is greatly beneficial. On the other hand, if you're assuming the worst about your partner's intentions, the conversation will not end well.

Ryan and Leah Dettmer walked this blurry line and came out stronger on the other side. Ryan has a freelance graphic design business in Miami and practices Muay Thai, a form of martial arts, weekly, and Leah works part-time and loves trying out new recipes for her four young children. There was plenty of blame to go around when it was time to share and compare their points of view. Ryan described his frustration when Leah invites her family to stay at their house without asking him first. Leah vented that Ryan never wants to "be the bad guy" and leaves her to handle all the discipline. "He always gets to be the fun parent," she said.

Taking time to think about what the other one wrote, and then talking a day later, allowed Leah and Ryan to process feedback before responding defensively. Even with this cool-off period, though, their conversations were tough. When we asked them how they persisted despite these difficulties, they said their excitement about their collective vision kept them going. If you need to, go back and reread that vision. Or take a break from the conversation and watch a funny TV show together. Or move into separate rooms and use an online tool to have a written conversation. Find what works for you, take another tack, and persist.

It might take more than one conversation to cover these matters well before you move to the next chapter. Take some time to collect your thoughts about what you learned about yourself and your partner from your conversations and what ideas you have for any changes implied by what you discovered.

We've given you much to do in this chapter. You may have had some uncomfortable realizations about yourself. You may have had difficult conversations. Either way, congratulations! We encourage you to find some fun way to celebrate having taken another step in your journey together. After taking a fresh look at the links among various aspects of your life and at your life with your partner, we hope you're now eager to examine connections with other important people in your lives.

PART II

YOUR WORLD

Chapter 4

ENGAGE YOUR CHILDREN

The novelist and essayist Ayelet Waldman has said that "there are times as a parent when you realize that your job is not to be the parent you always imagined you'd be, the parent you always wished you had. Your job is to be the parent your child needs, given the particulars of their own life and nature."[1] As we guide our children toward compassionate, contented, and confident lives, we face a leadership challenge: how to do so while at the same time investing in what matters most to *us* in other areas of our lives. Essential to this process is finding out what they need. If it's possible, asking them is the best way to find out.[2]

When he enrolled in our program, Luke Bailey had recently been promoted to chief technology officer for a large investment management firm, and his wife, Zoe, was on hiatus from her career as a teacher. When Zoe and Luke each sat down to talk with their children, they thought they knew exactly what each child would say. They figured Alan, their free-spirited six-year-old son, would tell them he wanted them to play more games with him or take him to Luke's pickup ice hockey scrimmages. He would thank them for being his parents and then ask how much longer he had to talk before he could play with his trucks.

Alan had a lot more to say than they had anticipated. Zoe had a ten-minute conversation with him over breakfast. Here's what she said about it:

> The main thing he was trying to convey was that his feelings— of fear, of sadness, of anger—may seem trivial to me as a grown- up but that he wants me to help him recognize them and he wants me to accept them. Of course, he didn't say it in those words, but that's the message I took to heart. I made a mental note that this kind of conversation must continue as he grows up from little-boy challenges to big-boy challenges. My role as his mother has to include listening so that I can give him the guid- ance and support he needs.

A few days later, Luke sat down with Alan at bedtime:

> His expectations of me involve spending time with him: helping him do things that he can't do, like carry heavy things, protect- ing him from bad guys, and not riling him up before bedtime. This last one especially was a surprise. I like to horse around with him. When I come home, the kids are usually on their way to bed and I'm pretty excited to see him, so I stir him up with my excitement. He's very self-aware—he realizes he has a hard time coming back down after this stimulation.

Zoe and Luke both started looking at parenting Alan a bit differ- ently. Zoe realized that when she told him not to worry about some- thing, or that it's not a big deal, she wasn't recognizing his feelings in the way that he needed. Following this realization, she made a point of echoing his feelings back to him by saying things like, "I can see you're frustrated now." She heard more from Alan about what was happening on the inside, enabling her to give him more of what he needed.

Luke realized that his guilt about coming home late fed his desire to have fun with Alan before he went to bed. But this wasn't meeting Alan's needs. So, Luke tried something new: finding a special chapter book he and Alan could read before bedtime. This allowed Alan to stay settled, and it became a cherished activity for just the two of them. Luke's guilt quotient went down.

We're going to invite you to have similar discoveries about your children. To lead well, you have to not only care about your people, but also maintain trusting relationships with them built on ongoing communication about your mutual needs and expectations. This takes commitment and skill, both of which you can increase to reap profound benefits. This is true in parenting, too. To explore this idea, let's start by considering in more depth what it means for you to be a mother or father.

See Parenting in View of Your Whole Life

While many of us would say that parenting is our most important role in life, few would say the parental role is the *only* important one. I (Alyssa) recall that one of my greatest fears prior to having children was that I would lose myself: the career identity I had forged, my hobbies, the close relationship with my husband, and other exciting parts of my independent life. While parenthood reshuffles our priorities and poses a risk of losing ourselves, it also creates opportunities to become more fully alive. The parenting life can conflict with the rest of our lives *and* it can allow us to enact our values, share them with our children, engage meaningfully in the other aspects of our lives, and make the world a better place.[3] After all, we're raising the next generation with the values we hold dear.

Pondering our roles as parents allows us to make smarter choices and act on opportunities for greater fulfillment. We're going to invite you to reflect on how being a parent, specifically, intersects with your life as a whole.[4] This will prepare you to talk with your children in ways that will increase your knowledge of who they really are, what they need from you, what you need from them, and how you can get better at leading them.

Career

How does your work affect your children, and how do they affect your work? Children, as I (Stew) observed decades ago, are the unseen stakeholders at work.[5] Our jobs and attitudes about our careers have a profound impact on our performance as parents and on our children's health and development. And the reverse is true, too.

At the most basic level, our careers and our children both need our attention. But how much is optimal? Despite some progress, there's still a widespread perception that the ideal employee is one who works the longest hours, answers texts and emails at all hours, and is available for travel or an extra assignment at a moment's notice.[6] While there is a growing recognition that longer work hours and more face time don't equate with better performance, this so-called ideal from a different era persists. And while having a full-time stay-at-home parent is no longer the norm, the expectation that a good parent—and especially a good mom—attends soccer games and school plays, prepares a nutritious homemade dinner nightly (to say nothing about packed lunches), and volunteers in the classroom also remains stuck in the popular consciousness.[7]

It's no wonder working parents today feel there simply isn't enough time to be effective in both roles—this zero-sum mentality is hard to shake. As Camila Orlov, who puts in long days at her company's LA headquarters, said, "I can't commute ninety minutes each way, work a full eight-hour day, and still be there to pick my child up from school by three. The numbers just don't add up." Camila isn't wrong; you can't be in two places at the same time, and when both parents work extremely long hours, it can take a toll on everyone.[8]

However, there are ways that work and family can be allies, not enemies.[9] By focusing on a lack of *time* for work and parenting, as most people naturally but mistakenly do, we miss the more nuanced picture of how these two parts of our lives can create value for each other. We're more likely to see how they can be mutually enriching if we look for such opportunities. The most obvious is that careers provide compensation and benefits that directly contribute to paying child-related expenses. Of course, for most working parents, a job is a financial necessity to provide food, clothing, and shelter. The other benefits a paycheck provides beyond these basics might seem to be just icing on the cake.[10] And yet this icing can have a profoundly positive impact on our lives, especially if it means our children can bond with nannies, discover in a tutor a kind of intellectual friend, or be able to attend truly special enrichment programs.

There's a growing body of research showing that, entirely apart from all the things that money can buy, the psychological fulfillment we gain in our work—confidence, a sense of accomplishment, a feeling of purpose—can make us better parents.[11] One workshop participant said this about going back to work after her maternity leave:

> If I'm being honest, the endless cycle of diaper changes, breastfeeding, pumping, and trying to get my baby to sleep is exhausting and somewhat mind-numbing. When I go to work and focus on solving a problem or finishing a project, I get a boost of energy and feel like I accomplished something. This allows me to come home and be with my baby without being resentful or brain-dead.

Mull this question: In what ways does your work make you a better parent?

You'll notice a flow of knowledge and skills between work and parenting if you look for it. One new father told us that "being a dad has taught me how to be patient and let the small things roll off my back. Before I was a father, every little glitch at work got me all bent out of shape. I've learned how to put things into perspective." This cross-training works in the reverse direction, too; the knowledge and skills we gain at work can improve our abilities as parents. Before deciding to stay home with her kids full-time, Amy Brenner worked in information technology services, a field she hopes to return to when her children are older. When they showed interest in coding, she used her work-related skills to create programming projects she could do with them. They started a family website that the children are responsible for updating. Amy is now thinking about starting her own company offering such tools to other parents. This kind of synergy is not limited to one industry or skill. Consider the negotiations we have or observe at work. In what ways do they inform how we navigate the complicated needs of our family members?

For better and for worse, our emotions don't turn on and off when we step into the office or into the house. Studies have shown that both positive and negative moods from work spill over into home life every day. Researchers found that on days when people were in a positive mood at work, they were more likely to be social and do fun things with their families in the evening. When people were engaged during work, they were more interactive with their families afterward and were more likely to spend time reading to children and less time watching TV.[12] The researchers calculated that, all other things being equal, this would equate to approximately 160 additional hours of "literacy nutrition" before entering kindergarten. The parents felt revitalized, too.[13]

Think about this: How does the emotional experience of your career influence your performance as a parent?

Attention is perhaps our most valuable resource—and is often overlooked in our unceasing obsession over how we divide our time. Regardless of where we are physically, the focus of our attention may

be elsewhere. This may mean simply *thinking* about our work
we're with our children or thinking about our parenting respons
ties while we're at work. However, we exist in a world where work
family are always accessible with digital devices, vying for our attention at all times of the day and night.[14] Technology may offer us all
kinds of new ways to successfully navigate the different areas of our
lives; however—and this is a big however—"techno-ference" occurs
when our interpersonal relationships are interrupted due to the use of
digital devices. The evidence is mounting that children are resentful of
parents' use of technology during parent-child time and that parents'
digital distractions have a negative impact on children.[15] We must be
hyperaware of this and erect smart boundaries.

Consider this: How does your accessibility to work demands affect
your relationship with your children, and vice versa?

Family

In marriages and long-term partnerships, having children changes
everything. First, the bad news: becoming a parent is associated with
lower levels of marital satisfaction, and as the number of children increases, satisfaction decreases further. Marital satisfaction declines
over time for couples without children, too, just not as steeply.[16] The
good news is that a decline in marital satisfaction isn't a foregone con-
clusion as a result of having children. Communication, coordination,
and conflict-management skills can help protect new parents from
these decrements.[17]

Coordinating responsibilities, negotiating who does what, and finding ways to spend meaningful moments with our partners are all much
more complex once children enter the picture.[18] This can become a
source of frustration and resentment. But it can also be seen as an opportunity to problem-solve together and try new things. When asked
how he and his wife make their demanding work lives jibe with their
roles as parents, Warby Parker cofounder Neil Blumenthal said two

words to Stew: "Google Calendar."[19] Of course, the answer isn't necessarily a program. It might be something as simple as deciding to say
grace at dinner.

One particular problem dual-career couples must solve is who takes
off work to care for a sick child. In one study of heterosexual parents
who worked full-time, nearly half of fathers perceived that this responsibility was divided equally between the mother and father. On
the other hand, only 35 percent of mothers felt this responsibility was
divided equally. (The majority of mothers saw themselves as primarily
responsible for doing so.)[20] In other words, regardless of the objective
division of who stays home with a sick child, there's often a perceptual
gap between people sharing parenting responsibilities.

Ask yourself this question: How is your relationship with your partner affected by how you allocate parenting responsibilities?[21]

Children also affect romantic relationships by altering the frequency
of emotional and physical intimacy.[22] One workshop participant told us,
"By the time I've worked a full day, put the kids to bed, and walked the
dog, I'm rarely 'in the mood' in the evenings. Sex feels like just another
thing on my already too-long to-do list." Her husband hardly wanted
to be the stereotypical husband complaining about not getting enough
sex, but he missed the old days when they made love several times a
week. On the flip side, raising children together connects people in new
ways beyond sex.

Consider this: How has your physical and emotional intimacy with
your partner changed in both positive and negative ways as a result of
being a parent?

Being a parent also demands adjustments as we interact with our
extended families. The number of grandparents providing childcare
has been on the rise for nearly twenty years.[23] When Jake Center and
Deena Altman, the Charleston-based couple raising two boys whom we
met in chapter 1, decided to try technology-free Sabbaths with their
kids, they didn't realize one of the toughest conversations they would
have was with Jake's mother. Although she didn't see the children that

often, she'd be on her phone and have the TV on in the background whenever they visited her. Deena and Jake had to talk to her about why they wanted her to be more psychologically present when she was with their family. Like Jake and Deena, many of us have to find new ways to engage with our extended family once we have children.

Lee and Grace Yang recently found themselves deep in the midst of an unexpected challenge—dealing with their son Adam's rare genetic disorder. Grace's parents moved in with them to assist in caring for Adam and his extensive medical needs, which was both helpful and frustrating. Lee said:

> I am so grateful for everything my in-laws do, like taking our son to weekly doctor's appointments, tidying the house, making Chinese family recipes from scratch, etc. At the same time, I am constantly frustrated because I really want to be our son's dad without having my father-in-law always telling us what to eat, how to buy milk, and how we should parent our son. We clearly rely on them so much, yet I want to be my son's dad with a grandparent supporting, not directing, my relationship.

Lee was reluctant to acknowledge his growing resentment because he's so grateful for his in-laws' support. And yet, once he was able to articulate his feelings, he and Grace were able to have a fruitful conversation with her parents about their relationship.

Think about this: How has the way you view your relationship with your extended family changed since you became a parent?

Community

Parents are not the only resources for meeting a child's needs. Whether congregations at church, neighborhood block groups, or ad hoc sports teams, our communities can suddenly be there for us when we least expect it. The realization that we can proactively build communities to support us is a game changer for many parents. Take a moment to consider the ways in which the different communities you are part of help you be a better parent. Also, think about how, conversely, being a better parent allows you to contribute to your community. I (Stew) take daily walks in a nearby park with one of my sons. We offer a word of greeting to everyone we meet and this, in a small way, brings our community a bit closer together while it gives me an opportunity to talk life over with my son.

Mull this over: How do your networks of friends, social and religious organizations, and other community resources enable you to be a better parent, and vice versa?

Self

Being a parent both influences and is influenced by the energy and attention we spend caring for ourselves—physically and mentally. As with the other parts of our lives, research has shown that nothing exists in isolation. Investments in sleep, exercise, and nutrition pay dividends on our children's well-being.[24] We've already mentioned how sleep deprivation can impair parental mood and decision making; it can even have life-and-death consequences for children, like an increased risk of serious car accidents.[25]

The benefits of exercise also extend to our children. Parents who exercise more frequently have children who are more physically active.[26] And, of course, our children learn a lot about food and nutrition from watching how we feed ourselves, not just how we feed them. In one not-so-surprising finding, when parents cared about healthy eating and exercise for themselves, their children were also more likely to eat the recommended number of fruits and vegetables each day, even when controlling for a number of other family-related factors.[27] Preparing homemade organic kids' meals while ordering a pizza and chugging beer may not help them or us.

Let's take a moment to discuss the messages we are sending our children about their appearance and weight. I (Alyssa) have had many conversations with other mothers about the body image problems we inherited from our own mothers and our desire not to pass those on to the next generation, particularly our daughters. The messages, explicit and implicit, we send to our children about our relationship to our bodies will influence how they think about themselves for the rest of their lives. My own strategy initially was to fake self-acceptance and a healthy attitude toward food and exercise in the presence of my kids. Doing so helped to shift my beliefs. When I talk about food as nourishment, praise strong bodies, and find fun ways to exercise, the message doesn't just get passed to my children; it also alters the way I see the world. I haven't totally gotten out of my old ways of thinking, but I've moved toward a healthier self-image than I likely ever would have if I didn't have children.

By caring for ourselves through stress-management techniques, mindfulness, and sheer downtime, we are better able to manage our emotions and buffer our children from the negative effects of stress.[28] Recent evidence demonstrates this. When parents practice mindfulness meditation, for example, their children benefit from an increase in positive parenting behaviors (for example, listening, quality time, and warmth).[29] Another study found that the more time mothers take for themselves to relax, the fewer behavior problems were observed in their children.[30]

Of course, children can be a source of inspiration and joy that directly enhances our lives. And while playing superheroes for a fourth straight hour might not be your idea of a good time, there's a reason they call it *childlike* wonder. Being a parent can connect us to our emotions and to the world beyond our own lives. It allows us to express our deeply held values, to build our legacy, and to experience wonder and joy on a daily basis. (See the box "Express What It Means to Be a Parent.")

EXPRESS WHAT IT MEANS TO BE A PARENT

Having thought about how being a parent fits with the rest of your life, take a bit more time now to articulate what you want from your role as a parent. Answer the following questions in writing, if possible.

As always, don't feel confined to respond in complete sentences. Use whatever creative ways you want to explore what you would like your identity as a parent to mean. Draw a picture, or create a sculpture, or dance the parent tango—whatever helps you to bring to mind your need for meaning as a parent.

1. Why did you become a parent?

2. What does it mean for you personally to find joy and fulfillment as a parent?

3. In what ways can being a parent allow you to live your values and vision?

4. How does being a parent help you engage in your career and in the community?

A couple of notes on expressing what it means to be a parent: in considering the reasons why you became a parent, you may have thought about the fun you want to have, the love you want to spread, and the legacy you want to leave.[31] If you're like many of the parents we know (and like us, too), you might find yourself feeling bad when parenting isn't sunshine and rainbows. Everyone feels this way. Everyone.

And just as you can love your job but dislike certain tasks, it is possible to both love being a parent and find aspects of parenting annoying or downright miserable. Most people go into parenting with expectations about how fulfilling it will be. They rarely anticipate the low moments. The disparity between the dreams and the realities of day-to-day parent life can often feel quite stark. So, as you move forward, it's wise, though difficult, to hold both ideas: parenting can be both sublime and abysmal, sometimes simultaneously. Keeping this paradox in mind can help you maximize the joy while letting go of some of the sense of failure you might feel when it sucks.

Know What Children Need

In exploring how our roles as parents connect to the other facets of our lives, particularly work, it's natural to focus on the inevitable tensions. We'll not ignore such conflicts, but we're going to emphasize the opportunities for changing our roles as parents that allow us to make things better in all parts of life. You may have already started to realize some instances where such possibilities exist, or can exist, in thinking about the questions we raised in the exercise "Express What It Means to Be a Parent." But it takes a bit more to get smart about spotting all the possibilities for synergy. To do so, you need to be clear about what your children really need from you (and what they *don't* really need) and how these interests fit into the big picture of your life and of your lives together.

We describe four categories of essentials for children, intended to help you home in on what your children require from you. We've culled these ideas from the vast literature on child development and offer them as guides.[32] For each category, think about your own children—their unique personalities, interests, aspirations, quirks, and difficulties. What does each one of them require to flourish? Differentiate what your children *need* from (a) what they *want* and (b) what you think you *should* provide. When you talk with your children about what they need from you, you might hear a long list of the things they want. We've heard plenty of children say they *need* more screen time, candy, and toys! Parents can also adopt beliefs about what we *should* provide for our children. We tell ourselves stories about what good parents do, and over time, it becomes difficult to differentiate those beliefs we internalize as a result of social pressures from the ones we hold independently, in our own hearts and minds.

Safety and Security

Feeling secure is at the forefront of our children's most essential needs. Obviously, children need to know that basics (for example, food, water, shelter, clothing) will be met. Beyond that, they deserve a sense of psychological safety and trust. They need to believe that we will care for them and return to them when we leave.[33] As they grow, feeling secure in their family relationships will allow them to take the necessary developmental steps toward independence.

Yet one of the most painful realizations of parenting is the fact that we cannot guarantee the health and safety of our children. Giving our children enough security to feel calm and confident, while acknowledging that bad things do happen, is a paradox of parenting. I (Alyssa) recently struggled with this when my children came home after practicing an "active shooter" drill at school. My then-eight-year-old son had a hard time falling asleep for several nights following that drill. Each night, he asked me to promise that nothing bad would happen to him or our family. I struggled to find a way to make him feel safe while also being honest that bad things, while highly unlikely, do happen. The thing I kept emphasizing is that he will be able to cope with whatever comes his way, and we will help him with that.

Values and Morality

Children learn about what matters most by listening to and watching us. Of course, our parenting isn't the only factor that determines who our children grow up to be—schools, neighbors, and popular culture play important roles, too. As does biology. But, to the extent we can, most of us want to instill our own values in our children as they grow into adulthood. Children start to internalize their parents' values quite early.[34] By the age of two, children show an understanding of right and wrong, the ability to show empathy for others, and a willingness to engage in behaviors to help those who have been harmed.[35] Parents affect their children's moral development through the advice they offer, the stories they tell, the conversations they have, and the way they talk about life experiences.[36]

Lisa Davis and Eddie McDonnell live in Denver with three children, ages nine through twelve. When they were creating their collective vision, Lisa and Eddie realized they wanted their children to see themselves as stewards of the environment. Yet this was rarely explicitly discussed at home, and Lisa and Eddie didn't deliberately practice ecological habits beyond basic recycling. They realized that if they want to transmit this value to their children, they needed to start talking the talk *and* walking the walk. They chatted with their children about why protecting the environment is important and brainstormed about steps they could take together to do so. Then they began an experiment: picking up trash during family walks—"hike and pick," they called it. Not only did this directly benefit the environment, it sent a clear message about what matters. They saw the benefits of doing their activity when one of their daughters said she was going to bring the idea to her Girl Scout troop.

Attention and Affection

Children flourish when they feel loved and appreciated for who they are. Development psychology research shows, for example, that eye contact, playtime, and reading together benefit children in the short and long run. We're talking about *quality* time.[37] Just because parents are physically in the same location as their children doesn't mean that children reap the benefits of attention and affection. It's the quality of the time that matters.[38] As children mature, the nature of their needs for your attention and affection shift, so your understanding of it should evolve, too. In fact, research has shown that overparenting (that is, helicopter parenting) can inhibit adolescents from developing their own leadership identity and confidence.[39]

Our ability to pay attention to work even when we are physically with our children—by connecting through digital devices but also by thinking constantly about work—makes the challenge of modern parenting more complex than ever. When Sabra and Aryan Kabir, the Israeli expats residing in Connecticut, sat down in their garden to listen to their children, they learned just how much their digital distractions upset the kids. Sabra told us, "Danya shared that it's hard for her that we spend a lot of time in front of our phones. She said she wishes our phones didn't exist. She also suggested that we put phones away from a certain hour of the day and have 'pure time' with her and with her brother." Pure time: What a great phrase!

It's interesting that they said this while sitting in a garden Sabra had spent much time cultivating, as if the beauty of that natural space had sunk in and inspired their words. These children were old enough to articulate this wonderfully. But it's important to keep in mind that children, especially younger ones—and no matter the setting—express their feelings nonverbally.[40] They may not have the language or the self-reflective capacity to say they want you off your phone, for instance. But they have other ways of letting you know how they feel. If a work-related call is interrupting dinnertime, the bedtime routine, bath time, time in the garden, or any other precious time, your child will probably express feelings about this to you. Perhaps he'll get loud, try to yank the phone away, imitate you on the phone, or repeatedly interrupt you. He may not say, "When you take that call, it hurts my feelings. It makes me feel as though I'm less important." Keep your antennae up for your child's nonverbal cues. Listen for hints.

Although many parents worry about how much exposure their children have to toxic technology, it's much less common for parents to look inward to explore how their own digital distractions affect their children. Aryan realized that, as the founder and CEO of a small medical supply company, he was constantly checking his phone for updates from work. Sabra saw that her phone was her connection to her family, work, and the culture that she missed in Israel. Hearing Danya and Adar so clearly identify their parents' addiction to their phones forced Aryan and Sabra to reflect on not only how much they relied on them, but also *why* they had such a hard time disconnecting. These deeper questions about where we devote our attention can help us to make lasting change.

Clear Expectations

Children benefit from clear expectations and consistent guidance.[41] We're not here to tell you what your expectations should be or how you should enforce them, except to say that ample evidence shows that corporal punishment does more harm than good.[42] Beyond that, however, surely it's up to you and your partner to determine the expectations you have of your children, whatever they might be, and provide guidance about them so that your children eventually develop the capacity to regulate themselves. Some of the parents in our workshops realized they weren't sufficiently developing their children's need to learn responsibility and autonomy. It's no surprise, then, that one of the more common experiments parents in our program undertake is developing a "chore chart" for their children. This serves the benefit of both clarifying what is expected of children and teaching them what it means to contribute and to be responsible, with positive ripple effects—mainly by freeing up time—on parents' work, community, and private selves. (See the box "Catalog What Your Children Need.")

We encourage you to read through what you wrote and push yourself to think even more deeply about each child's distinctive needs. Think about the different kinds of things your children require from you and to try to provide at least one example from each of the four categories.

CATALOG WHAT YOUR CHILDREN NEED

Take the time now to write about what each of your children needs at this point in their lives, recognizing that this will shift, of course, as they develop. This is a chance to question your assumptions about what your children really require. In other words, do your best to differentiate what *you* think they need from what *they* want. Consider, also, how well you're meeting their needs. It's fruitful to take stock of how things are going right now to identify opportunities for growth and improvement. Leaders, remember, deal with reality and try to make it better.

On your own, think through each of the four categories described earlier (safety and security, values and morality, attention and affection, clear expectations) for each of your children, and compose your notes about what you think each child needs, in light of any unique circumstances in their lives.

Start by responding to the following prompts:

We've said it before—parenting is hard. And while our children don't come with an instruction manual, there are a lot of resources available for parents whose children follow typical developmental patterns and have age-appropriate needs. However, for children with special needs, whether they are physical, cognitive, or emotional, the process of uncovering what they need at any given point in time is exponentially harder.

You don't have to know how to do this on your own. Indeed, you can't. It's a good idea to take advantage of professional support in whatever capacity it might be available to you, be it in-school social workers, occupational therapists, licensed clinical psychologists, or nonschool,

1. What does each of your children need to feel safe and secure? How you can best prepare them to develop the self-reliance to navigate the world? On a scale of 1 (poorly) to 10 (fully), where do your efforts currently fall?

2. What does the collective vision you created in chapter 2 reveal about your priorities for the values you wish to instill in your children? What behaviors do you want to model to teach them about what matters most to you?

3. What does each of your children really need in terms of your attention and affection? Would they benefit more from thirty minutes of your full attention or three hours of your divided attention?

4. To what extent are you being clear with each of your children about what you expect from them? On a scale of 1 (not at all) to 10 (completely), how clear and consistent are you?

community-based or private resources. In chapter 6, we'll give more guidance on how to build a community of support, whatever your children's needs, including dealing with illness and other unforeseen problems.

Get on the Same Page About Your Children's Needs

An essential part of this book is getting on the same page with your partner in parenting. This means discussing your beliefs and assumptions and seeing the other person's perspective. Research has shown, not surprisingly, that when parents align their approaches and collaborate effectively, there is a measurable positive influence on children.[43] This alignment is especially important for parents who are separated or divorced, where finding common ground and establishing respectful dialogue may be particularly challenging.

Anthony Aceto, a newly appointed judge, and Joyce Casano, a senior marketing manager, live in a small house in the suburbs of Atlanta with Mario, age five, and Clara, age two and a half. We asked them to reflect independently on what each of their children needs and to review one another's perspectives. There were some things they agreed on: Mario would benefit from a consistent bedtime routine; Clara needed some time with her parents without her big brother around. But there were also some disagreements. Joyce said, "Anthony holds Clara to the same standards that he holds Mario to, even though she's three years younger. When she throws a fit or won't listen, he doesn't seem to understand that Clara is no different than Mario was at that age. Expecting her to behave like a five-year-old isn't fair." Anthony saw it quite differently. He said, "Joyce babies Clara too much and lets her get away with stuff. I think Joyce is a little too soft-hearted because Clara is our last baby, but I don't think it's doing Clara (or us) any favors."

Of course, Anthony and Joyce weren't thrilled to hear about how the other perceived their respective approaches to Clara's behavior. But it started an important conversation about how to handle Clara. It helped them understand why they were each acting the way they were, cleared the air of some grievances they had been holding on to, and allowed them to see opportunities to get on the same page. From there, they were able to agree on a reasonable approach that they could both implement when Clara threw a temper tantrum. While Clara didn't magically stop throwing temper tantrums, Joyce and Anthony felt a lot less stressed when a tantrum did happen because both agreed on how they were going to handle it. (See the box "Seek Common Ground About Your Children.")

SEEK COMMON GROUND ABOUT YOUR CHILDREN

Find some time to sit down with your partner and discuss each of your children in turn. Share what you each think they really need from you. Ask each other questions, clarify your understandings, and push your partner to explain what they mean. As always, listen with an open heart and mind. Help each other by keeping an eye out for *wants* versus *needs* and *needs* versus *shoulds*. Try to reach a common understanding of what each child really needs from you. This is also an opportunity to share what each of you dreams of getting out of being a parent.

Write down your hopes for your children and your relationship with them. And describe how you want parenting to fit into the broader picture of your lives.

Even when you approach this process with a willingness to see the other's perspective, there will likely be some disagreements about what's best for your kids. You may come from different cultural backgrounds or different upbringings—or you may have different philosophies of parenting. Regardless of why these disagreements emerge, it's important to be compassionate in how you address them. There are a few different options. First, there's the compromise—no one gets exactly what they want, and you just pick something in the middle. If you think your children should visit their grandparents every weekend, but your partner thinks that's overkill, a compromise is pretty straightforward. Simply agree to visit them every other week.

In other scenarios, though, this sort of mathematical averaging doesn't work. Fatima Masood, who was raised in a conservative Muslim household, wants her daughter to start participating in *hijab* (including wearing a headscarf) when she turns fifteen in a few months. Ali Masood thinks their daughter should decide for herself what to do. Neither Fatima nor Ali wanted to compromise. In scenarios like this, consider what alternatives might work on a case-by-case basis. Is it an agree-to-disagree situation? Can you ask your children for their opinion on the matter? Can you try out different approaches and reflect on what works best? Can you seek the input of another trusted person or an imam, priest, or counselor? Seek creative ways to address these roadblocks and find what works for you. Fatima and Ali talked with their daughter about what hijab means to each of them and discussed each of their perspectives. They're still working on how to navigate their religious and cultural traditions as a family, but the dialogue is much more open and constructive now than it was before.

To the best of your abilities, come to a shared understanding where you can, and if you need to agree to disagree, revisit those situations often.

Before you talk to your children, think ahead about how your children will hear what you say.[44] Consider both what you want to talk about and how you want to approach the conversation. The main purposes of these conversations with your children are to:

- Develop a shared understanding of the values most important to your family.

- See things through the eyes of your children.

- Lay the groundwork for ongoing conversations about these topics.

The way you prepare will naturally differ depending on the age and personality of each of your children. While we can provide some suggestions for how to engage with children at different ages and stages, you know your children best. Pick an approach, and even a time of day, that seems likely to work, but be open to having a few conversations to find out what actually works.

Talk About Values

You have already identified the values that are most important to you and explored them in your collective vision. Now, consider how you want to describe these values to your children. For toddlers, this might be less a dialogue and more a repeated sentence you share as a family. It might be something along the lines of, "In our family, we are kind, we have fun, and we love each other." In our (Stew's) family, the constant refrain was "Everyone's different," which signified our interest in treating each person in a way that respected their idiosyncratic needs. You could do an art project together with this phrase at the center and post it on the fridge to encourage repeated discussions. Or pick a few children's books that emphasize particular values you want to teach and read them regularly.[45]

For elementary-school-aged children, you might ask them to talk about how we treat ourselves, how we treat each other, and how we treat our planet. You can gather their input and add the values you'd include in those categories, too. At this age, remember to use language they'll understand. For example, instead of saying that you value "justice," you might say that you value "treating people fairly." It would probably help to have some of this vocabulary sorted out before you start your conversations. For adolescents, consider providing them with a printed list of values beforehand and ask them to rank the top five values of the family. You could then use it as a prompt to compare responses, similar to what you did with your partner.

Whatever the right approach is for your children, the most important part is that they feel that they are part of the family's conversation about values and that it is something you can revisit over the months and years ahead.

See Things as They Do

To achieve the purpose of these conversations with young children, you might ask a question like, "What do good moms and dads do?" or

"What do you need from us to grow up happy and healthy?" For school-aged children, focus more on understanding what they think you expect of them and what they expect from you. You can prompt different aspects of their lives that will make sense to them with questions like, "How can I help you succeed in school?" or "What do you need in order to keep your body healthy?" For adolescents, you can discuss the expectations you have of one another. Ask them to describe what they believe you expect from them and listen to what they expect from you. Depending on your children, this might be an opportunity to tell them what you expect from them and what you think they need. And again, children often convey their feelings through their behaviors. Part of looking for the answers to your queries lies not in just listening to what your children might say or noticing their failure to respond, but in decoding their behavior and hearing what they're trying to convey with their actions.

Lay the Groundwork

Much of this is just good parenting, but we're encouraging you to think of these conversations in a new context, so that they will extend your understanding of leadership and so that you'll see how leadership skills enhance all areas of your life. These conversations with your children should set the stage for more talk about how things are going, what they need, what your mutual expectations are, how you will work together as a family to live shared values, and what all this means in the context of your lives beyond your family. These conversations should be forward looking, hopeful, and optimistic. If your child tries to rehash the wrongs done by you (or if you start to do the same), refocus the conversation about the possibilities of moving forward together. This is a chance to get your children excited about the prospect of doing things in new ways. Later in the book, we'll go through what it takes to figure out smart new ways you might try.

TALK WITH YOUR CHILDREN

Have conversations with each child and write down what each one said. Stay attuned to their nonverbal behaviors. Examine your insights emerging from those exchanges. What did you learn about what your children need from you? What assumptions did you have that you discovered aren't exactly accurate? What could you do differently as a family? How would you approach this conversation next time?

Then, discuss what you heard and what insights you gained with your partner. If you spoke with your children separately, give your partner a sense of how the conversations went and what each child said.

For now, in these conversations, your children might benefit from warming up to the idea of trying new approaches as a family. Raise their enthusiasm by asking for their ideas about things *you* could try to do differently. Again, this question has to be broached in an age-appropriate way. For younger children, you might ask, "What could we try together to practice [insert a value you discussed here]?" For older children, you might ask them to take some time to create a few feasible suggestions for ways you could more closely live your values as a family and to share them with you in a few days. (See the box "Talk with Your Children.")

Here are a few additional recommendations as you prepare to have these conversations with each of your children:

- **Make time to talk to each child without siblings present.** Although it might seem convenient to initiate this conversation at a family dinner, pressure from siblings to act or feel a certain way might inhibit openness. That's not to say that you can't, over time, have these conversations about family values over the dinner table; it's just that we would recommend starting with one child at a time.

- **Decide whether you and your partner will be together when you have each conversation or whether you'll have them one-on-one.** Regardless of which option you choose—and there are pros and cons to both—it is helpful for you both to be on the same page before either of you have these conversations. Then compare impressions and insights afterward.

- **Consider when and where you want to have these conversations.** For some children, bedtime might be when they're finally calm enough to have a conversation while you snuggle together. Others are cranky in the evening and can barely put together a sentence. For older children, you might consider asking them to suggest a time and giving them some advance notice of what you're going to be talking about. "I need to talk to you about something" probably sounds pretty ominous, so try saying, "I have some ideas I want to get your thoughts on."

- **Take notes during the conversations or spend a few minutes right afterward jotting down what you heard.** This will help you process what you learned, discuss it with your partner, and refer back to it in later conversations.

Discover Your Children Anew

These conversations don't always go according to plan, and that's OK. First, some children are more verbal, articulate, and introspective than others. Second, children can be distracted, moody, hesitant, or confused. None of this should be surprising if it's the first time you've asked them to communicate in this way. One of the main benefits of doing this sooner rather than later is to make these kinds of conversations normal. Treat this as one of the many conversations you can have about your lives together. If you're frustrated with how one or more of the chats went, cut yourself some slack. Was your first job interview your best interview experience ever? Probably not. Think of this as part of your journey; you're discovering anew, all the time, what it means for you to lead. The only failure here is the failure to learn. You will likely get many more chances. And remember, your child's responses may not be expressed in words.[46]

Joyce Casano and Anthony Aceto decided that they would each speak to their children one-on-one, taking turns on consecutive evenings before bed during what is normally story time. They thought about how they wanted to approach each conversation and mapped out a few questions they both wanted to ask. Their conversations with two-and-a-half-year-old Clara were, unsurprisingly, rather one-sided. She was able to articulate that she wanted playtime and cuddle time with them, but that was really the extent of it. Still, they felt good that they each got to spend some quality time with Clara without her big brother, something they saw as an important need for her earlier in this process.

Their experiences with Mario proved more interesting, which they each told us about. From Joyce:

> I broached the conversation by asking, "What do good mommies and daddies do?" Mario replied, "Take care of people and love them." I asked him if he thought I was caring and loving, and he agreed. I was a bit surprised by his answer to what things I do that he likes. He said he likes it when I work from home because he can see me. I was always torn about this, because being present doesn't mean I'm "present." When my children see me work, it also means they see my stress, which is more prevalent lately.
>
> I realized they also see my focus, work ethic, and confidence, which is positive. More importantly, when I finally do check out

of work, I'm instantly focused on them versus having to wait for a (in some cases, long) commute. When I asked him what good sons do, he listed a bunch of very specific things that, while true, are not the most important, so I emphasized that good sons listen to and respect their mothers and fathers, because if children listen to their parents, their parents can keep them safe. I ended the conversation by letting Mario know that he can always talk to me about his feelings.

When Anthony tried to ask Mario the same questions, his conversation didn't go quite as smoothly. Anthony told us:

From our conversation, I did gain a sense that Mario cares for me. But it is hard to have a meaningful discussion with a five-year-old. He didn't really answer my questions, and it was hard to get him to focus. According to him, he likes school and is glad that I send him. He is also excited about trying Little League in a few weeks and the prospect of going to camp this summer for the first time. While it didn't tell me much about our values or parenting approach, I feel good that he can share these positive feelings with me. We are slowly making progress.

When Anthony and Joyce reconvened to discuss their conversations with Mario, they were each surprised by the experiences the other reported. Anthony was amazed that Joyce managed to get Mario to answer her questions. Joyce was surprised that Anthony had so much difficulty. They discussed whether there were differences in how they approached Mario, or whether they just caught him in different moods. They made a plan to have the next conversation with Mario together. Anthony and Joyce also discussed Mario's comment about liking it when Joyce works from home. They talked about the pros and cons of doing so, both for Mario and for Clara, but also for Joyce's career and her well-being. After discussing a variety of options about when and where

Joyce works, Joyce decided to try working from home on Wednesdays each week. She planned to talk to her boss about this arrangement and, if she received approval, to try it out for a few months—looking at the impact on herself, her family, and her work.

In reflecting on their conversations, Joyce and Anthony solidified their belief that Mario doesn't really know what's expected of him in terms of listening and being respectful, and that he would benefit greatly from some straightforward guidance. They decided that they would work together to come up with a few clear guidelines. If he could understand them, they would have a foundation to go back to when behavioral problems surfaced. Joyce and Anthony emerged from this process with some new ways of looking at their roles as parents in the greater context of their lives. They also identified a few things that they wanted to try to help meet the needs of the children while also fulfilling their own goals as parents with lives outside the family.

One more point about engaging your children in dialogue: they may respond differently to different parents, in part because of what the parent brings to the conversation in ways the parent might not even be fully aware of. It's useful to ask yourself whether you were anxious about the talk. Did it feel awkward? Was it hard for you to address feelings? Were you feeling guilty? Did you feel unprepared for these chats? Whatever emotions were stirred, your child was probably picking up on them. And while we may not be able to change the way we feel as readily as we're able to change the way we act, it's useful to give some thought to what's inside. If you know you're feeling anxious or awkward, it may be helpful to say, "I know we haven't done this before and it may be a bit weird for you; I know it's a bit weird for me." What a great way to model for your children that it's OK to talk about feelings, right there, in the here and now.

Chapter 5

CONNECT WITH COLLEAGUES

The people in your career network—bosses, colleagues, subordinates, clients, investors, former coworkers, sponsors, and mentors—are also part of your network as parents and partners. The ripple effects of your relationships in your career have a profound effect on other facets of your life, and that is true whether you work a traditional nine-to-five job, are a self-employed freelancer, have managerial responsibilities, have no direct reports, or have stepped out of the paid workforce for now. And vice versa.[1]

Grace Yang is an analytics manager at a large consumer goods firm. As we described earlier, her son, Adam, has a rare genetic disorder, which prompted her parents to move in with her and her husband, Lee. She had had what she thought was a difficult performance review three months earlier. While participating in our workshop and engaging in conversations with important stakeholders, she had a conversation with her boss, Jeremy. Grace was happily taken aback to learn that Jeremy thought she was ready for a promotion and, perhaps more importantly, that part of his calculus was the way she's been managing her son's illness, as she reported to us:

I wrestled with whether or not to bring up Adam. I don't usually bring up his condition. I'm scared I'll be put in a "downgraded" career box. But I bit the bullet and mentioned Adam's illness to Jeremy. I was happily surprised to hear that, in light of Adam's special needs, Jeremy respects my contributions to our business even more. He said I've learned, faster than most, what really matters in life. He added that he hadn't been sure about whether or not to ask about Adam. I told him that my son is my favorite subject and I'm always happy to talk about him. Things were going so well that I even told Jeremy about a fundraiser I'm organizing to raise money for medical research for Adam's illness. Now Jeremy's looking into how our company can become a corporate sponsor!

Grace had been operating on the assumption that her colleagues viewed Adam's illness as a career disrupter, so she had hesitated to bring it up at work. She had not realized that Jeremy might see it as an element of her growth. This talk gave both of them an opportunity to clarify assumptions. Jeremy had been reluctant to bring up Adam because he respected Grace's privacy. Grace reassured Jeremy that it brought her joy to talk about her son.

Reflecting on this conversation, Grace realized she had been avoiding Jeremy because she was afraid of rehashing the feedback she had gotten in her previous performance review. In taking the initiative to clarify, however, she learned that she was doing better than she had thought. What she had perceived as criticism of her earlier performance was actually Jeremy's attempt to point out ways she could prepare for a promotion. Further, Grace recognized this fear of criticism as a pattern that pops up in other aspects of her life.

She drew further insights from other such conversations, which were all triggered by a desire for her and her husband, Lee, to improve as parents. We'll find out more about how Grace and Lee used this knowledge to make their lives better. And we'll address how institutional policies can solve parts of the puzzle. But, for now, let's focus on what you can do as an individual and as part of a parenting partnership to cultivate supportive relationships around your family, while at the same time gaining insights about parenting in view of your whole life.

Partners in parenting have to be aligned with each other and with their children, but they must also strengthen the web of social relationships in which their families live. The aim always is to gain knowledge of what you and people outside your family need from each other, mainly through ongoing conversation. This will allow you to find creative ways to meet these needs while remaining mindful of your collective vision. You're going to be surprised to discover that you have more support—more freedom to pursue that vision—than you think.

Navigate Relationships with Bosses

Handling authority relationships can present the thorniest of challenges. There are limits to the influence we may have over our managers (or supervisors, or bosses, or whatever title you use). But most people have more power than they imagine to mold this relationship.

Direct managers play a critical role in how we experience work in connection with the rest of our lives. In one fascinating study of working parents, researchers showed that parents who felt their supervisors were supportive of their lives outside work were less likely to have work stress on a given day spill over into family life that evening, even on days when their work was highly demanding.[2] Managers can thwart or facilitate our desire for work that matters, plays to our strengths, and enables us to feel good about ourselves and, indirectly, about our lives as parents. Family-supportive managers often play a more important role in employees' work-life experiences than family-friendly policies themselves.[3]

Managers are also gatekeepers to certain employee benefits. Policies such as flextime (changing *when* we work), telework (changing *where* we work), and part-time work (changing *how much* we work) are often applied at the discretion of managers.[4] So managers can function as arbiters when it comes to reshaping our lives.

Sometimes managers give official permission to use a specific policy to support life outside of work, but they accompany it with insinuated cues about negative repercussions, such as being delayed for promotion or targeted for layoffs.[5] Similarly, decisions managers make about scheduling (such as calling late-afternoon meetings that interfere with childcare pickups) and expectations they convey (such as immediate responses to emails at all hours) can cause major disruptions to our lives as parents, often without those managers even recognizing their impact.[6]

On the other hand, managers can help provide creative solutions— often going beyond official organizational policies—for managing the relationship between work and family.[7] Practices that address the unique needs of individual employees have become known as "i-deals," which researchers have linked to improved performance and well-being.[8] They can serve as role models by demonstrating that it's normal to have harmony and a rich identity outside of work. As a Chicago lawyer recently told one of us (Alyssa), "My boss was the first man in our department to take a paternity leave. It sent the message that fatherhood is important to him, and it made me much less nervous about taking paternity leave when my first child was born." Bosses can go a long way in creating an environment of sensitivity and respect for employees' out-of-the-office lives.[9]

But there's often a tension between wanting to impress bosses with our work ethic, capability, and commitment, and wanting to bring the whole self into the workplace.[10] The push and pull between "looking good" and "being real" can leave us unsure about how to talk to bosses about other commitments. As an example, let's say at midday your manager asks if you're free for a meeting at 6 p.m. If you want to create the impression you are fully committed to your job, you might say, "Sure, no problem!" On the other hand, a more honest response might be, "I can make it if it's really important, but I'll have to scramble to see if the babysitter can stay late" or "I can make it if I have to, but I was hoping to spend some time with my child today."

If we want a manager to think highly of our commitment to our work as a traditionally ideal employee, it's tempting to go with the "sure" option. Most of us might not articulate the latter option verbatim, but it might be helpful to know that there are costs to keeping our thoughts and feelings hidden. Workplace "acting" has been shown to cause stress as well as strain—emotional exhaustion, psychosomatic complaints, and negative effects on marital partners.[11] Conversely, research has shown that being free to be yourself with your boss (within limits—no one wants to hear *everything* on your mind) boosts engagement at work, reduces stress, and lessens symptoms of physical illness.[12]

One of the most important conversations you can have to improve life for your children is the one with your manager. Just as you spoke with your partner and children to understand more about what you all need from the relationship, find time to have a conversation with your manager that helps you gain mutual understanding, build trust, and generate ideas to make things better for *all* parties, just as Grace did.

These conversations should *not* launch with how your work has to accommodate your family life. Such zero-sum thinking (good for me, bad for my boss) is what we're trying to diminish. It's also not the best strategy for getting what you want for your family. Instead, set out to discover more of the truth about what you need from each other. Seek to uncover inaccurate assumptions you and your boss might be making that hinder your performance at work and your life beyond it. Then, if it feels right, explore ways to improve your contributions at work that produce positive results elsewhere.

One conundrum people face when preparing for a conversation about mutual needs with a manager is how much to reveal. Gender may affect the way people respond to bringing personal our lives to the office. Stew (as a man) is more likely to gain a "fatherhood bonus" from talking about his family. Men with children tend to be perceived as more responsible and committed compared to men without kids.[13] And they even get a boost in their pay.[14] On the other hand, Alyssa (as a woman) might be susceptible to the "motherhood penalty" that women with children incur, which can dent opportunities for advancement and raises.[15]

The good news is that even if you keep your conversation entirely focused on your professional life, you will reap greater mutual understanding of your values, aspirations, and expectations by talking with your manager about what you need from each other. Recognizing that there's no one right way, take some time to consider how you might approach this conversation. Ideally, at the end of this conversation, your boss will be thinking that you know her better and care more about what she's trying to accomplish than before you spoke.

If you're reluctant to open a dialogue with your manager—or if you question whether a conversation like this could help strengthen your web of support—we understand. For now, if you're nervous about initiating a dialogue with your boss, just concentrate on gaining a greater awareness of your manager's expectations, goals, and values, and allowing them to better understand yours. Accomplishing this alone will be a win for you both. In the background, try to keep in mind all you've been discovering about your role as a parent who leads. Again, more knowledge and greater trust are the goals. Don't push to change anything other than how much you know about each other. Try to remain open to discovery.

Have the conversation with your manager in whatever setting has the highest chances of undivided attention. Let them know your purpose—to clarify your mutual needs—and start with your perspective: "Here's what I think is important to you [then list the top three or four]. Do I have it right?" Relentlessly seek to comprehend what matters most to them, with follow-up questions about specifics. Be ready for surprises, including that your boss expects fewer and somewhat different things from you than you had previously thought. That is a common outcome of these conversations, though sometimes the opposite occurs, of course. In either case, having a better grasp of reality boosts your ability to forge the future you want because you can address things as they are, not as you might wish them to be.

Then, reverse it: "Here's what's important to me in my role at work [list the top three or four]. Does this seem right to you?" Check for understanding so you both reach a clearer picture of what will make your relationship successful in the days ahead. And, if (but only if) it seems like it might be helpful, raise possibilities for making changes that would benefit you both, perhaps based on any mismatches you've uncovered in this dialogue. (See the box "Talk with Your Boss.")

Your conversation with your manager will be different from Grace's, of course. We find that people take away uniquely practical insights from these conversations. More importantly, they open the door for more consistent, open communication in the future. That's true even when conversations are in some ways disappointing.

Camila Orlov, Peter's wife, the retail executive struggling with her long commute in LA traffic, had a two-hour conversation with her manager, Nazir. She tried to talk to him about her values and goals in her career. It didn't go well. Camila told us:

> He made me sound like a cog in a machine. As we discussed expectations, he just kept focusing on my need to scale the business. I started on this team approximately ten months ago, and a small group of us managed to launch a very successful multimillion-dollar business for the company. Now his expectation of me is that I will help him scale it. He didn't focus on, or even allude to, me as a person. It just turned into a laundry list of the things I need to do.
>
> I know that I needed to be open to whatever he had to say. But I came home annoyed. I put so much into my work, my time and effort, but I'm not treated like an actual person. I let other areas of my life suffer at the expense of work, and this has really made me question it. It made me think more seriously about shifting out of this role to work with a different manager. It also made me reconsider pushing myself to work so many crazy hours when my efforts aren't appreciated.

TALK WITH YOUR BOSS

Prepare by thinking about your direct supervisor and write down your thoughts, ideas, or feelings in response to the following prompts (and if you have no supervisor, just skip this exercise):

1. What do you think your manager expects from you?

2. In what ways are you overdelivering on what they need from you?

3. In what ways might you need to step up your contributions?

4. How well do you think you're meeting expectations? (Recommended: Use the same 1-to-10 scale you used with your children, 1 = poorly, 10 = fully.)

Now, consider the flip side of this relationship:

5. What do you want and need from your manager?

6. How well is your manager meeting your expectations? (Use the 1–10 scale.)

Think about the approach you'd like to take in ensuring that this exchange will be a win for your boss. How is it going to benefit them? Choose a location for meeting that will increase the odds of this being the outcome, whether it's in an office, at a coffee shop, on a walk around the neighborhood, or somewhere else. And what would be a good time of day or week to have this conversation, from your boss's point of view?

As soon afterward as you can, write about what you learned. Look especially for assumptions you had that turned out to be correct or not. Consider how your perspective shifted as a result of this conversation. Did any ideas emerge for four-way wins down the road?

Camila may not have liked what she heard, but it gave her useful information about what her manager values. It allowed her to question whether her long work hours were worth it and opened her to the possibility of finding a different position. As we talked with Camila, we reminded her that one conversation does not define this entire relationship. Her boss could have been feeling exceptional pressure from his higher-ups that day, or maybe he didn't understand what Camila was hoping to get out of the conversation. While we certainly encouraged her to consider other options, we also reminded her not to place too much stock in one interaction. She reluctantly agreed and actually learned something else about herself—when people let her down, she's pretty quick to write them off. So, there was another layer of growth in self-awareness that came from this less-than-pleasant experience.

As novelist and civil rights advocate James Baldwin said, "Not everything that is faced can be changed, but nothing can be changed until it is faced."[16] As in all our important relationships, we have to ask ourselves, would I rather know the truth or not? Leaders try to change reality for the better. Whether your conversations are agreeable or dispiriting, you've shifted toward understanding the important people surrounding your family and to building relationships that help you pursue your vision. This understanding, as well as taking the initiative to have the conversations, is part of your growth.

Send the Right Message to Your Direct Reports

If you are in a managerial role in your organization (that is, supervising others), the research we reviewed earlier about the role of managers in our work and nonwork lives is especially relevant. You are a role model, and you make decisions that affect the lives of your employees. The way you help your direct reports find purpose in their work, and the messages you send, can have lasting impact on your people and their families. If you don't have direct reports at this time, either skip this section or read for future reference.

Of course, the people you supervise influence you, too. When you establish trusting, high-quality relationships and empower them to succeed, you reap the benefits: not only will they perform tasks better, they'll be more willing to exceed their job requirements to support your team and the organization.[17] You actually increase your own likelihood of success. You enhance your reputation as someone who inspires commitment and you develop relationships that you enjoy. It's a virtuous circle: trusted subordinates allow you to delegate with relatively little worry, which gives you greater bandwidth at work and more freedom to make positive changes for your own family and personal life.

Think about the people who report directly to you—their goals, capabilities, and interests. Think about what you need from them to do *your* job well and to find joy in *your* life. Consider the messages you might be sending about your expectations. You've probably talked about these expectations in performance evaluations. While, of course, there are benefits to mandated performance evaluations (meeting legal and staff planning needs, for instance), managers often assume they suffice to communicate information, drive performance, and encourage employee development. But, conversations about expectations and goals can—and should—happen in various contexts. And evaluations are not always good conversations, anyway; they are often constrained by preconceptions of what good job performance looks like. It can be useful to think outside of an evaluation and find additional ways to focus on an employee's values, vision, and purpose, perhaps in a casual venue, like over coffee or during a walk outside.

Remember that your goal is to set up conversations in which you clarify what you and an employee need from each other. You want to open the door to wins for your organization but also for both of you beyond work. These conversations allow you to discover what others expect from you (correcting, if you weren't quite right beforehand, your impression of what you *think* they need). They also allow you to brainstorm about mutual gains. You might learn, for instance, that one of your direct reports is eager to take on a responsibility you now have. For her, it would be a developmental experience that she'd be excited about doing; for you, it would free up time to focus your attention elsewhere. This presents an opportunity to try a new way that's good for her, for your organization, and for you. Depending on the number of direct reports you have, it might not be feasible to have such conversations with all of them right away. But start now, while you are feeling the momentum. And keep the momentum going.

Emma Lopez, the management consultant with two young children, set aside an hour to talk with David, one of her direct reports. In advance of the conversation, Emma told us that "David is quite possibly the nicest person you'll ever meet, and also one of the hardest working and most ethical." She added, "I know how hard it will be for him to provide anything other than extremely positive feedback. So, getting him to admit areas where I might be able to better support him will be a stretch." When she asked David what he needed from her, he said he wanted her to continue to lead by example, to provide guidance on engaging with difficult clients, to be a problem solver in sticky situations, and to act as both an expert and a sounding board. As Emma anticipated, David was effusive about her qualities as a team leader. To her surprise, though, and without prompting, he followed the compliments with a suggestion. Emma said:

> The one piece of "constructive" feedback he shared, in his kind way, was about demonstrating a better example of "balance." He said that while I never impose my crazy work schedule on the team, they do observe my late nights and weekends, and it makes them worry about me and wonder if they'll be able to "swing it" when they get to my level at the company. I'm not sure I had thought about my habits that way before.

Emma was able to see her role from a new perspective and to re-examine the inadvertent messages she was sending. She had assumed that she was doing a good job keeping her private life private, but she realized that she was speaking volumes without actually saying any-thing. She had assumed that her team needed to see her commitment to her job. The conversation with David led Emma to consider the pos-sibility that her "crazy work schedule" wasn't doing as much good for her team as she had thought. Plus, if she stopped responding to emails and doing work at all hours of the night, she might actually have time to watch some TV with Marcos as they did in their pre-kids days.

Like Emma, consider each of your direct reports, or at least a repre-sentative two or three. It's useful to keep in mind that you are in a posi-tion of power when you engage with your direct reports, so take care in how you talk about work and the rest of life. For instance, while you might disclose that you are pregnant, it's not a good idea to ask whether your direct report is. Focus the conversation on goals and values with the explicit aim of helping your people bring their whole selves to work. Again, start with what you think they expect of you and then ask, "I'm sure I don't have the full picture. What am I missing?" This makes for a more psychologically safe social context for honest exchange.[18] Ideally, after each of these conversations, your direct reports will feel you know them better and genuinely care about them as people, rather than view-ing them as cogs in a machine. When you combine these insights with those that have already emerged from conversations with your boss, your partner, and your children, you further expand your way of seeing things, and in doing so, new ways of doing things. (See the box "Talk with Your Direct Reports.")

Find Support Among Coworkers

Our interactions with colleagues, outside of those in a direct report-ing line with us, can be sources of inspiration, camaraderie, and col-

TALK WITH YOUR DIRECT REPORTS

Think about your direct reports and write your thoughts, ideas, or feelings in response to the following prompts about each one:

1. What do you think your direct report expects from you?

2. In what ways are you overdelivering on what they need from you?

3. In what ways might you need to step up your contributions to help your direct report?

4. How well do you think you're meeting expectations? (Recommended: Use the 1–10 scale, 1 = poorly, 10 = fully.)

Now, consider the flip side of this relationship:

5. What do you want and need from your direct report?

6. How well is your direct report meeting your expectations? (Use the 1–10 scale.)

As before, give some thought to location, timing, and whatever else you can do to make this conversation beneficial for *both* of you. And, again, when you're done, write about what you learned and note especially any ideas for innovation that came up.

---

laboration in ways that supervisor–subordinate relationships might not be. Many organizations also have an employee resource group specifically focused on connecting parents.[19] (These aren't always what you need: some can lean more toward narrow definitions of parenthood, like welcoming only mothers or heterosexual parents. Others can be more gripe sessions than empowering ones that might, say, offer skill development and interpersonal support.)

At their best, relationships with our colleagues can motivate us at work, and they can also take on a life outside work. But they can also take on a less positive role in our lives, as sources of competition and frustration. Most of us have experienced the nasty effects of a coworker who has in some way, consciously or not, tried to undermine our reputation for the sake of their own advancement. There may be no way to turn around a relationship with an obstinate or narcissistic colleague. But some of these minefields can be avoided if we cultivate work relationships in ways that help us express our values and achieve our goals.[20]

Emma's husband, Marcos Lopez, the army veteran and an investment manager, set out to have conversations with two of his work colleagues, Terrance and Oscar. Terrance is a little more junior than Marcos, but they're not in a direct reporting relationship. They've worked together for more than two years. According to Marcos, Terrance was initially hesitant to reveal what he wanted from the work relationship:

> But as our conversation continued, Terrance praised my ability to keep our work in perspective, to break down the more complex requests we receive into something actionable, and to be there as a sounding board. After I probed a little, he said I could be more open and animated. We both get tasked with pulling together complex sales presentations with tight timelines and with little to no warning, and work becomes incredibly stressful. Terrance doesn't see this process affecting me (it does), nor does he understand how I pull it all together "seamlessly" (I've never experienced a seamless process). I think he's right: if I talked more about what I was doing and why, people would see that it's rarely seamless for me either. I'd probably get more support as a result.

Next, Marcos spoke with Oscar, who started around the same time as Marcos and is at a similar level. Marcos told us:

> I had a less formal conversation with Oscar over dinner. Oscar recently moved into a sales role within our company. So, we don't work directly together anymore. When I asked him what his expectations were of me, he said, "This, this right now." Oscar elaborated and said I was the person he trusted to ask questions and that he had selected me as a mentor because I was generous with my time and candid. I never really considered myself as a mentor to Oscar because I'm no further along in my career than he is.
>
> When I asked what I could do differently, Oscar recommended that I be willing to ask for help when I need it. He thinks that I take on more responsibility than most of my sales team members, but don't ask for assistance. That's helpful feedback. I have a hard time asking for help for two reasons. One, I love solving problems myself. At times, this can make things take longer than they should, especially when there are subject-matter experts available to help. Two, I feel like asking for help is a sign of weakness, even though I gladly offer to help everyone.

Marcos enriched his relationships with both Terrance and Oscar as a result of these conversations. He also learned about himself. He realized that his "show no weakness" approach might have served him well during his military career, but, in his civilian life, his colleagues are looking for him to be more open to sharing his experiences and receiving support. It was liberating for Marcos to imagine not shouldering everything himself and trying to make difficult assignments look easy. Asking for help allowed him to streamline his work, work smarter (not harder), be more of a team player, and have more time to spend with his family. Showing vulnerability at work enhanced his work relationships and taught him how to open up to people he had kept at a distance.

Reach Further Out

Just as our career paths are not limited to the jobs we currently hold, our career network is not limited to those we work with on a day-to-day basis. This is particularly true for people not in traditional employment (for example, freelancers, entrepreneurs, artists) or for those not currently in the paid workforce (for example, stay-at-home parents, people between jobs). And while the term "networking" often connotes meaningless and awkward schmoozing, it can and should play a positive role in our careers and lives.[21] Think of your network as a web of support that can help you move toward greater fulfillment in work and greater harmony in life.[22] This sort of support doesn't emerge from passing out business cards or connecting on LinkedIn (although there's nothing wrong with doing either). Instead, cultivating these relationships requires intentionality. Consider the broader array of people who can help you reimagine your work and your life.

When we talk about strengthening our career networks, a key element is the presence of mentors. Mentors are often treated as the cure-all for any and all woes. Not sure about your next career move? Talk to your mentor. Stressed about your workload? Talk to your mentor. No time for family? Talk to your mentor. Research has demonstrated the benefits of mentoring to both mentees (in higher compensation and greater career satisfaction) and mentors themselves (in increased job satisfaction and higher performance).[23] As a result, organizations have latched on to the notion of mentoring programs.[24] While getting an assigned mentor can be helpful for people newly entering organizations or roles, formal mentoring programs can short-circuit the exploration of what mentoring should look like and how to get or be a mentor.[25]

One assumption we frequently make is that we just need to find one mentor, and once we find that person, we're done with the process of building mentoring relationships. This assumption limits us to a narrow scope of support, often relying on a single person to be a catchall adviser for all of our career-related needs—whether venting frustrations, identifying next steps, introducing us to clients, or helping us strategize about ways to find greater harmony between work and parenting. Even if there were a single person who was skilled at doing all of these things, it's a lot to ask of a single person. And it poses a risk to you, too; when you rely on a single person to be your source of career wisdom, you're relying on one point of view, which may or may not reflect the reality of your life and career. And don't just stick with the default person to whom you might have been assigned; think broadly about the types of support you need to help you understand the role that work plays in your life. Then consider the wide array of individuals who might be well suited to support you. This could include former coworkers, college friends, the parents of your children's friends, or people you follow on social media whose careers you admire.

This book collaboration is a result of Alyssa, then a recent college grad, taking a long shot on emailing a scholar (Stew) whose work she admired in 2005. Stew wasn't a boss or a colleague—he was someone in the wider circle of her field. That outreach has led to more than a decade of academic collaboration that has enriched us both.

Don't fall into the trap of thinking that proactively seeking to build such relationships is selfish. We assume that mentoring is a one-way street—they give and we take. It's not surprising that people often feel icky about the prospect of networking. When we challenge this assumption and consider our own contributions, these relationships become more meaningful. For example, when a senior person like Stew throws Alyssa's name in the ring for new opportunities, this helps him build his legacy and enhance his long-lasting impact. Both of us benefit, though in different ways.

For the past six years, Amy Brenner has been a stay-at-home parent to her two children, Bethany, thirteen, and Connor, eight, and a frequent volunteer at their school. Now that they are becoming more self-sufficient, Amy and her husband, Jack, talk about whether and when Amy might want to go back to work. But these conversations happen infrequently, and they never lead to any specific action. When we asked Amy to reach out to people in her career network, she wasn't sure who to talk to besides Jack. Eventually, she settled on catching up with her former colleague Julia from her IT days. The two had occasionally reconnected over the years. Amy took the train into DC from their home in Potomac, Maryland, for lunch with Julia, who has steadily climbed the corporate ladder in the company where Amy used to work. In reflecting on the conversation that ensued, Amy said:

> The more we talked, the more I realized I didn't want to go back to work at a big company. Sitting behind a computer in a cubicle all day just does not appeal to me anymore at all. Even the idea of part-time or freelance IT for a corporate employer doesn't excite me. I realized that I'd like to try something new, maybe something more creative, or maybe I'd like to start my own business. I'm in the fortunate position where I don't have to generate a big income for my family, so I can take some risks. Julia and I bounced some ideas off of each other, and she suggested that I talk to her in a few weeks after I explore some of these ideas. Now I feel like I have some homework to do, but I'm looking forward to doing it. Julia got pretty excited about some of these ideas, so maybe there's even a way for us to collaborate.

The conversation with Julia helped Amy clarify what she *didn't* want to do next and helped ignite enthusiasm for possibilities to come. She felt creative afterward. Rather than feeling as if she was a drain on Julia's time, she felt as though Julia was engaged in supporting her.[26] Spending a few hours that week doing some homework on potential ideas while her children were at school not only rejuvenated Amy, but made her feel better about the time she had taken away from work to raise her children and more optimistic about the ways she might approach work and family moving forward.

Unlike Amy, who left the workforce entirely, Sabra Kabir moved to freelance consulting in the insurance industry when she moved from Israel to Connecticut in order to support her husband's entrepreneurial venture. The freelance work allowed her to contribute to her family's income and keep her mind sharp, while also allowing her to create a schedule that worked for her family. It even gave her time to swim laps most days. However, Sabra had pulled back from working with one of her most frequent clients, Uri Halevia, a senior executive for a major Israeli government agency. Sabra sensed that the projects she contracted with Uri were frequently outside her area of expertise and came with expectations for incredibly quick turnarounds. Yet without those contracts, Sabra felt as if she wasn't working as much as she hoped to, and she missed both the income and stimulation. Rather than just continuing to turn down the work that Uri offered her, she decided to start a conversation with him to see if she could renegotiate expectations and find a way to collaborate. Sabra said:

> I told Uri more about the reasons I frequently turned down consulting gigs with him. He got a bit defensive and said that it was up to me to manage my boundaries better and to redefine the terms of the contract if they didn't work for me. While I didn't like feeling like he was blaming me, I did realize that I have more power to renegotiate the terms of the contract than I realized. I was looking at it as a take-it-or-leave-it situation—as though I had to turn down the opportunity or accept it and then just smother feelings of resentment if it didn't go the way I wanted it to. So, I guess that's a good thing . . . I have a suspicion that Uri might not be enthusiastic about me pushing back when it actually comes down to it. But, it's worth a shot to see what happens.

Both Sabra Kabir and Amy Brenner pushed themselves outside their comfort zones to build support despite their nontraditional career

TALK WITH COWORKERS AND OTHERS IN YOUR CAREER NETWORK

Who are the people in your career who are part of your vision of the future? Take some time to think about all of the people who are, or could be, nodes in the web of support you need around yourself and your family. Draft a list of a half-dozen and note why each one is important to you. Think about the ways you believe you are important to each of them. Are you surprised by who shows up on this list? Why?

Unlike bosses and direct reports with whom you might conduct regular performance reviews, relationships in your broader career network risk stagnation unless you take the initiative to stay connected, create trust, and cultivate understanding about how you can help each other. Pick a couple of people with whom you could have a conversation now about your relationship. Start with expressing gratitude by explaining why they mean something to you. Indeed, if you do nothing more than this, they will undoubtedly feel good about you and about themselves.

But there's so much more to gain. Let them know what you think they need from you, and then, as ever, ask what you're missing in this picture and persist in gently asking for details. Learn about what they're thinking, taken in the context of all the insights you've gleaned so far about your vision and the people populating it. Do the same basic preparation you did with your boss or direct reports. Consider your mutual expectations, rate how well you are meeting one another's needs on the 1–10 scale from 1 (poorly) to 10 (fully). Think about what you can do to make things better.

As soon as you can after the interaction, write down—or record a video or voice memo on your phone—your reactions to the conversation. What did you learn from it, and do you have ideas for how you can contribute to strengthening this relationship? Bonus points: reflect on how you prepared for this conversation and what you discovered about how to make such exchanges fruitful and fun.

paths. You, too, have freedom to advocate on your own behalf. Crafting your career and building supportive relationships can open doors for you to be more present, engaged, and fulfilled with your children and partner.[27] (See the box "Talk with Coworkers and Others in Your Career Network.")

There are innumerable opportunities to enrich your life—as a parent and in all the things that matter to you—by strengthening relationships with people in your professional life. But most people usually don't think this way, because the default mindset is to assume a zero-sum relationship between work and the rest of life. Our hope is that the conversations we've invited you to have in this chapter have expanded your thinking about how to make this idea come alive for you and your family.

Chapter 6

CULTIVATE YOUR COMMUNITY

The ancient African adage "it takes a village to raise a child" may have become part of our modern consciousness, but few people actually feel part of a village. In the United States, we remain centered in our nuclear families, with less connection to extended families and local communities than ever.[1] Americans today feel there are few people with whom they can discuss important matters.[2] Yet, as ever, parents need all kinds of assistance in order to garner the resources—quality childcare, flexible work arrangements, emotional support, and much more—they need to raise their children while contributing to the world through work.

While his wife, Amy, was considering how to reinvent her IT career after staying home for a few years, Jack Brenner felt that he was smoothly sailing in his career as the director of technology at the Bureau of Land Management. Amy and Jack have two children, Bethany, thirteen, and Connor, eight. They have become friendly with a few parents of their children's friends, happily chatting when they run into each other at school and taking turns hosting playdates and sleepovers. But at the time they took our workshop, they hadn't made much effort to strengthen those relationships. In fact, since having children, they hadn't given much thought to friendship at all, let alone how they might develop deeper friendships with other parents. As a pair of introverts, making plans with other couples didn't come naturally. We challenged them to reach out to their community. Here's what Jack had to say about a dinner they recently had with another family:

> After struggling to sync our schedules, we finally had dinner with Kayden and Hyun and their two kids. The conversation turned to how we're juggling the various responsibilities of our lives. It felt good to hear that they have similar challenges. Hyun recently returned to full-time work, but, like Amy, she had spent several years full-time at home.
>
> Kayden has to travel frequently, and we recently helped them out by picking up their children from school on a day when Hyun couldn't get there. They told us how much that meant to them. We agreed that having the kids play together was good for the kids and having this "support group" was good for the adults, so we made plans to keep it going.

For Jack and Amy, this dinner conversation transformed how they thought about their relationship with this other family. While it was hardly an inconvenience for Jack and Amy to help with school pickup, they hadn't realized how much it meant to Kayden and Hyun. This realization, along with the support-group vibe of the dinner, made Jack and Amy want to actively support Kayden and Hyun. They felt encouraged to ask for help when they needed it and looked forward to the upcoming dinners where they could vent, laugh, and strategize together.

Parents striving to lead together have to be aligned with each other, their children, and their coworkers, and they must be deliberate about strengthening a wider web of social relationships. This chapter will advance your knowledge of what you and the people in your community (including your extended family) need from each other. Ongoing conversations will help you find practical and creative ways to meet these needs while remaining mindful of where you want your lives to go.

Strengthening social connections within communities and extended families can help us feel connected to the world and provide more sense of purpose in our daily lives. Friends, neighbors, and compatriots can be powerful sources of support—emotionally, logistically, and educationally.[3]

The concept of "community" might seem fuzzy at first glance. Your definition will be determined by your understanding of who, besides your colleagues and your immediate family, matters to you. The community relationships most salient for working parents tend to be friends, childcare providers, teachers, neighbors, and members of religious, political, or social groups. Here we'll explore the value of attending to these often-neglected relationships. Then we'll plunge into the thicket of our extended families that, for the sake of convenience, we bundle up in the domain we refer to as "community."

Define Friends and Neighbors

When one of my (Stew's) children developed a serious mental illness as a young teenager, our family was thrown into chaos as we struggled to cope. Were it not for the emotional and logistical help given lovingly by friends, neighbors, local school teachers and staff, our religious community, and colleagues, it would have been impossible for us and our children to find a footing in a world turned upside down. Mental health professionals played a role, too.

We all accrue dramatic benefits from our social relationships. These benefits range from decreased susceptibility to the common cold to greater overall satisfaction with life.[4] In a landmark study that followed 724 teenage boys from the 1930s to the present day, researchers showed that close relationships are one of the essential factors for maintaining physical health, cognitive sharpness, and mental health into old age.[5] It even enhances longevity.

Friendships allow us to develop trust and find acceptance and support. This is *social capital,* a term researchers use to describe the benefits we get from the people in our networks.[6] While this may sound rather self-serving, we all know the benefits of having friends come to our aid during difficult times, and we know how good it feels to help others.

A large body of research demonstrates the importance of social capital in virtually every aspect of our lives: our own health, our children's academic achievement, even our ability to find jobs.[7] It's not the number of friends that matters so much as the quality of those friendships. A few trusted friends can add as much, if not more, meaning to our lives than a gaggle of amiable acquaintances, particularly as we get older.[8] Yet being a parent, especially with young children, is associated with both having fewer friends and spending less quality time with them. A 2015 Pew Research Center report indicates that half of parents rarely or never turn to friends for parenting advice or support.[9] When the transition to parenthood is accompanied by a reduced investment in friendships, we miss out on a powerful source of support in all areas of our lives.

Jennifer Todd is a second-grade teacher in Minneapolis. She is also divorced and mother to a twenty-two-year-old son, Zach, and a fifteen-year-old daughter, Brianna. Unlike many parents who find their friendships dissolving once they have children, Jennifer found that a group of moms became her lifeline, especially when she realized that her then-husband could not truly be her partner in parenting. These women, mothers of kids in her children's school, represented an array of work and family situations (married and divorced, gay and straight, in paid work full-time, in part-time employment, and not working outside the home at all). Yet they shared a common commitment to support one another through the struggles of parenting and the rest of life. Jennifer sees them as her true partners in parenting—the ones that she can turn to in the commotion, confusion, and joy that is working single parenthood. Even though her children are older, these women are still part of the fabric of her life, and her children's lives. She recounted to us how Brianna recently asked several of these moms to talk about their career paths as she considers what she might like to study in college.

Friendships are different from other close relationships. Unlike with parents and siblings, we get to choose our friends, so they often possess qualities we value but don't find in our family of origin, like a shared interest in jazz, a passion for hiking, or a commitment to a political cause. Our friends can also offer a fresh point of view as a result of a distinctive cultural or religious heritage. Friendships are no doubt affected by the psychological baggage we bring from our childhoods, but we might be less likely to revert to archaic habits of interacting with friends than with family members. In addition, we can have a variety of kinds of friends, all at the same time. Our life partners are often expected to be lovers, best friends, co-parents, and financial partners, but there's usually less pressure on friends to perform well in so many roles, so friends are often better in serving as impartial sounding boards.

Many of our closest friendships are with coworkers. Most full-time employees spend about half of their waking hours at work, so this is no surprise.[10] Indeed, friendships at work can facilitate greater engagement and happiness in and out of the office.[11] But workplace friendships come with their own set of complications. When lines blur between friends and colleagues in the workplace, we can be distracted and experience tensions between the personal and the professional, inappropriate interactions, and a slew of other interpersonal challenges.[12] As a result, workplace friendships require a special degree of consideration and careful communication.

For this reason, it's important to cultivate friendships outside the office. Because many of us feel we don't have time for friends, we can overlook opportunities to cultivate them. Think broadly about friendships you might like to grow. Think about friends whom you don't talk to nearly as much as you'd like to. Think about people you spend time with but don't really know all that well (like your neighbors or the parents of your children's friends). Imagine people you haven't met yet. Perhaps a friend has a friend who has children about the same age as yours.[13]

Buoyed by the great dinner that he and his wife, Amy, had with Kayden and Hyun, Jack decided to invite Mitch, the father of one of his son Connor's best friends, to meet for coffee.

> Amy has a few moms that she gets together with regularly, but I felt weird inviting a dad out for coffee. Amy has become friends with Mitch's wife, and they text each other to arrange playdates or carpools. I usually just rely on Amy and I didn't even have Mitch's phone number. Once I texted him, we met for the first time without kids. We ended up talking a lot about the Cub Scouts, since our boys are in the same troop, admitting that we avoided getting involved because we didn't want to get sucked into too many activities. But we hatched the idea of planning activities together so that neither of us had to be responsible for everything. Mitch likes to fish, so we talked about starting with a fishing activity for the troop. As we were talking, I learned that Mitch works in the professional area that I would like to go into after I get my MBA. Mitch offered to connect me with some people in the industry when I'm ready. It just felt good to get to know him better.

Jack went from seeing his friendship with Mitch as something that just existed whenever their wives arranged a get-together to building his own friendship and realizing that such a relationship could enrich his life. Moreover, Jack realized he could let go of the idea that it was weird for dads to get together for coffee, but normal for moms to do so. When we reflect on our assumptions, we open new pathways to meaningful connections that we might have ignored. (See the box "Identify Friends and Neighbors.")

IDENTIFY FRIENDS AND NEIGHBORS

Write down the names of your friends and neighbors. If it helps jog your thinking, sort them into categories (for example, parents of your children's friends, friends you've lost touch with over the years, people you'd like to get to know better, coworkers you consider friends, etc.).

From this list, identify a few friendships from this list that you would like to strengthen, relationships that could add greater fun or meaning to your life if you invested in them. Your partner in parenting can offer helpful insight as you think about friendships. Here are questions we suggest you talk over together:

1. What would you want your friendship with this person to be like?

2. In what ways can you enhance this person's life?

3. What has held you back from investing in this relationship in the past?

4. What are ways that you could give to this relationship that fit with the rest of your life?

Honor Childcare Providers and Teachers

A reality for working parents is that our children often spend as many, if not more, waking hours in the company of childcare providers as they do in our care.[14] This need not be a source of guilt. Research suggests that while there is demonstrable evidence for the benefits of parental leave immediately following the birth of a child, over the long run, there are no cognitive or emotional differences between children with a stay-at-home parent and those who have other forms of childcare.[15]

This underscores the important role that nannies, babysitters, daycare providers, and teachers play in the development of our children. For most readers of this book, the village that supports our children's growth is no longer a network of extended family and friends living communally. Instead, nonfamily, paid childcare providers help hold our lives together. High-quality childcare is associated with higher academic achievements and fewer behavioral problems into adolescence, and most of us will select the highest-quality childcare available within our particular constraints.[16] It's essential to establish trust in these relationships. Doing so benefits our children in the form of a shared understanding of their needs. It can benefit us, too.

Eddie McDonnell, a financial analyst, and Lisa Davis, a senior communications manager, live in Denver and both have demanding careers. Lisa also has a side hustle as a photographer, selling her work online and participating in local art shows. They rely heavily on their new live-in nanny, Mya, to help care for their three children, ages nine, eleven, and twelve. For an exercise in our workshop, they sat down with Mya just three weeks after she started on the job. They asked her how things were going. Lisa described her response this way:

> I was surprised to hear she thinks we don't like her. She said that because we don't talk to her very much, she assumes we don't like her. This gave us the opportunity to explain to her that we are introverted and that talking a lot just isn't our style. We explained that we do like her and we think she's doing a great job. It's crazy to think she would have just gone on thinking we were mad at her if not for this conversation.

Eddie added that the conversation also gave them the opportunity to talk with Mya about their expectations for their children's diets. "We told Mya how important it is to us to incorporate fruit, vegetables, and protein in the kids' meals," said Eddie. "Since she's making a lot of the meal decisions on her own, sharing the value we placed on healthy eating and giving her guidance made us feel a lot more confident that we're all on the same page."

Lisa and Eddie learned that even in just a few short weeks together, assumptions and habits were already developing that could be easily clarified in a conversation. They did not fully realize Mya's vital part in making working parenthood viable until after thinking, writing, and talking about it in our workshop. It's now plain that by nurturing their relationship with Mya, they are better able to trust her to impart their values to their children. This leaves them less stressed about their children and freer to focus on their work.

Conversations like these need not be limited to those who provide full-time, live-in childcare. And they should not be considered onetime events. Taking the time to get on the same page with teachers, occasional babysitters, coaches, and dance instructors allows us to feel more connected and supported. This, in turn, enables us to give our children what they need while still devoting attention to our work. I (Alyssa) had to take a break from an important writing project to speak on the phone with the director of my son's summer theater camp. After a rough first day, we talked about how we could both help my son get through the remainder of his time at camp and allow him to grow from the experience. I was more confident that we were all on the same team working to support him, rather than fretting about how I could "fix" the problem before the next day of camp. So, I was able to go back to my writing to finish what I'd started (this chapter!).

And it's mutual: sharing our perspectives with those entrusted with nurturing our children enables our childcare providers and teachers to feel more connected to us and gives them a clearer picture of the value of their efforts. They do a better job when they know what we care about and that we value their input and perspective. The children of engaged parents have higher self-efficacy, intrinsic motivation, and mental health, which undoubtedly makes teachers' lives better, too.[17] This doesn't mean you need to become a helicopter parent, volunteering to chaperone every field trip or running the Parent Teacher

Association. In fact, overinvolvement can create excess demands on you and overwhelm your children.[18] And, it should go without saying, generally overworked teachers and caregivers do not benefit from constant input from parents about how to manage each child's every need, wish, or sensitivity. Choose thoughtfully the ways you interact with the people who care for your children; don't just do so reactively, when a problem arises or a parent-teacher conference is scheduled. (See the box "Acknowledge Childcare Providers and Teachers.")

ACKNOWLEDGE CHILDCARE PROVIDERS AND TEACHERS

Consider the people who care for your children—teachers, nannies, daycare providers, coaches, school counselors, tutors. First on your own, and then with your partner, give some thought to the following questions about them. As ever, taking notes gives you a useful reference when you talk to them later.

1. What are some quirks (for better or for worse) about your child or family of which your caregivers should probably be aware?

2. What's the best way to communicate with caregivers that respects their boundaries but opens the door for talking about complicated topics?

3. Which relationships are most central to the well-being of your child and the functioning of your family?

4. What role, if any, do these caregivers play in supporting your family's values and imparting them to your children?

Bijan Nazari is the finance director of an international nonprofit organization and a single father with one daughter, Esther, age nine. After reflecting on the questions in the exercise "Acknowledge Childcare Providers and Teachers," Bijan realized he was disconnected from his daughter's school experience. When he asked Esther about school, he didn't get many details beyond that it was "good." Parent-teacher conferences were months off, so Bijan, as part of his work in our program, decided to schedule a phone call with his daughter's teacher, Mr. Bloom. Bijan described the conversation and its impact:

> We spoke for about a half hour. After learning more about
> Mr. Bloom's goals for the class and sharing my desire to feel
> more involved in Esther's school life, Mr. Bloom suggested that I
> could come into the class to share a story. I realized that talking
> to the students about my recent business trip to Nigeria would fit
> perfectly with their social studies unit on world cultures. I went
> to the class, read a Nigerian children's book that I brought home
> as a gift for Esther, and talked to them about the history of the
> country, its people, the food, important cultural ideas, and my
> work there. The class loved it, and my daughter did, too.

Seek Out Members of Community Organizations

Connections around us can help us share our values with our children. Many of us have cobbled together a community over the years out of a hodgepodge of relationships with friends, neighbors, teachers, and others. It's a good idea to invest thoughtfully even just a bit in strengthening, broadening, and deepening those relationships.

Yet, most of us still overlook opportunities to enlarge our communities. How about joining a village that already exists? Is there an existing group of people who share similar values and who are likely to care about you and the well-being of your family? Organizations like local political parties, libraries, professional networking societies, or sports recreation leagues often do a lot of legwork for you by organizing social events, providing on-site childcare, or offering educational programming for members. Religious congregations can provide educational, social, emotional, and logistical resources.

Ken Hubbard, a former Navy Seal, and his wife, Ashley, recently moved to Montreal so that Ken could pursue a full-time MBA. Ashley works part-time while providing primary care for their one-year-old daughter, Ava. Ken and Ashley are Catholic and attend Mass every Sunday. When we spoke with Ken about his church involvement, he said:

> We treat church as a time and place to connect with God. My wife and I both had experiences in our past where we were criticized for not participating in more church activities, like going to Bible study and being on committees. We were reluctant to revisit that experience, given our recent move, me starting my MBA, her starting a new job, and us having a young child. So, we just went to Sunday Mass and then left.

And, while Ken and Ashley felt spiritually fulfilled, they realized that in their new life in Montreal, they were a bit isolated, far from family and friends. Despite the reluctance that grew out of past experiences, Ken decided to speak with their priest, Father Joe, about how they might become more integrated into the church community. After this conversation, Ken said:

> I was surprised by how much more supportive and open-minded Father Joe was than the priest of the church I attended in Virginia Beach. He offered suggestions on how we might participate more without overextending ourselves. He encouraged us to attend the next church family social and reassured me that we shouldn't feel any obligation to do more than what works for

us. I'm feeling excited about making friends with children who aren't in my MBA program.

Once Ken and Ashley identified how their past experiences shaped their assumptions, they were able to explore the possibility that things could be different at their new church. Their conversation with Father Joe was a reassuring first step in realizing that church could be both a source of spiritual fulfillment *and* a community of support.

Religious organizations aren't right for every family. For some, belonging to a cultural heritage group or volunteer organization with a mission that is aligned with your values—a group that cleans up a nearby park, or one that supports refugees, or one that empowers women—might fit the bill. Finding such organizations might take some research and a bit of trial and error. I (Alyssa), for example, thought that becoming active in my homeowner's association would be a great way to get to know my neighbors and feel more embedded in my community. I found myself in the middle of an ongoing feud about when and where dogs should be allowed off-leash that added unnecessary work and drama to my life. Not every effort aimed at meaningful community engagement will be a success!

Adults who volunteer their time for charitable causes report better health and psychological well-being, particularly for those who begin such activity feeling socially isolated.[19] Adolescents who are engaged in their communities feel more empowered, are less likely to take up risky behaviors, and are more likely to be thriving several years down the road.[20] They are also more likely to remain civically engaged into adulthood.[21] Helping others clearly helps us, too.[22]

Even if working parents claim they don't have time for relationships in their communities, they can find that this is one of the most powerful ways to generate four-way wins. From signing up for a neighborhood improvement association, to contributing to the church's white elephant sale, to joining the local cat-rescue brigade, to tutoring immigrant kids, the parents we've worked with have found that such activities have,

BRAINSTORM COMMUNITY ORGANIZATIONS

Revisit the values and vision that you composed in chapter 2. Think about how they could be enhanced through building connections to your community. Brainstorm types of organizations that might help you to do so. Some might be obvious: if you wrote that you envision your children as "proud of their Chinese heritage," it's not a stretch to imagine that a Chinese family neighborhood club might be a good fit. In some instances, it might take a little more reflection to identify organizations or clubs that would help you express a particular value or goal. For example, if you wrote about "helping those in need," what organizations might offer the kind of help you'd like to get involved in—is it a domestic violence shelter, a food pantry, a local hospital, or something else?

Choosing a path will likely take some further conversation (about who you collectively want to help), some research (about organizations in your area), and some creativity (about how to feasibly fit in such an activity). Some internet sleuthing will reveal options that might be available. In collaboration with your partner in parenting, talk over which community organizations you might investigate. Keep things flexible at first. Know that just because you explore an opportunity does not commit you to further involvement.

1. Of all the organizations you've brainstormed about, which fit best into your lives in the future? Prioritize two to four relationships in your community that you'd like to deepen.

2. Are these relationships best pursued by one of you, both of you together, or all of you as a family?

perhaps paradoxically, created a feeling of time expanding. Training your mind to see community engagement as nourishing, and not consuming, is possible when you think about how such activities benefit your family, your work, and yourself. Community activities can help you bring your values to life. In doing so, you can create opportunities for greater peace, harmony, and fulfillment. (See the box "Brainstorm Community Organizations.")

Take In Extended Family

Relationships with people in our families of origin are often fraught. For Grace and Lee Yang, relying heavily on Grace's parents as live-in caregivers for their son, Adam, was a mixed blessing. Lee was reluctant to open a can of worms by speaking with his in-laws about their mutual needs because of how much he and Grace relied on them. Yet when Lee did finally speak with his father-in-law (the more challenging of his in-law relationships and the one who caused most of Lee's angst), he said:

> I have more insight now into how and why he became who he is. His own father died when he was young, and so, as the eldest son, my father-in-law had to assume a great deal of responsibility. This comes naturally to him, and he likes doing things for others and feeling important. But he is not quick to praise and can be very critical.
>
> In the past, when I heard his criticism, I felt either annoyed or defensive. With this new appreciation of who he is, I had better understanding of where he's coming from. This past weekend he praised me for fixing our faucet (which I certainly appreciated) while also pointing out some problems. Instead of saying to myself, "Why are you being critical?" I realized this is just who he is. I listened and acknowledged what he was saying. Many times,

his points just don't make sense to me, but sometimes I can learn from them.

While this conversation didn't fundamentally change Lee's father-in-law, it changed Lee's interpretation of his father-in-law's words and actions:

> Instead of thinking "he should be minding his own business" or "he should let me parent my child," I've come to accept the bad with the good. This is who he is and I am trying to acknowledge his comments without as much emotion. I value a lot of what he does and have also articulated that I need space to do things, too.

By stepping back and reflecting on his relationship with his father-in-law, Lee became more compassionate and felt a bit more serene.

Grace Yang had found herself in the difficult position of trying to maintain the peace between her father and Lee, while protecting Adam from tensions. Before speaking with her father, Grace said, "I've been worried that my parents are burning out, as there's been a mention about how they've put their life on hold since Adam was born. I was expecting to hear my father criticize my long work hours, Lee's passive-aggressive attitude, and our parenting." Grace spoke with her father:

> My dad assured me that I'm meeting his expectations and that his wishes are to (1) have more quality time with me because he'd like me to share more of my thoughts with him and (2) allow him to stick close to me and my brother, including taking a vacation or two with time spent apart during the vacation. It was liberating to hear that he's actually pretty satisfied right now with our relationship. We also agreed that if I share more of my thoughts and he disagrees with me, it's OK. At least we will have talked about it so we understand each other.

Between my conversation and Lee's, the whole atmosphere in our house has shifted. I'm so much calmer now that I'm not constantly worrying about the tensions between Lee and my dad. I'm much more lighthearted around the house. It has also dramatically improved my relationships with my dad, Lee, and our son, Adam. And I'm clearly more relaxed and focused at work as a result. My coworkers have noticed and told me so.

Having children adds a new layer of complexity to relationships with our extended families, who are often integral to the functioning of our lives as working parents. Yet when our parents become grandparents to our children, and our siblings become their aunts and uncles, the shifting of expectations can set even the warmest and most stable relationships on edge. Connections with our in-laws, who we might be used to seeing infrequently, change when grandchildren arrive. Everyone has an opinion on child-rearing, and it's often a bumpy transition for grandparents, who have to realize they aren't in control. Of course, adding children to an extended family can joyfully enliven them in magical ways, too, as the circle of life turns before our very eyes.

Relationships with siblings, too, are often a mix of love and strain.[23] The quality of our sibling relationships matters; they have been shown to have an equally strong impact on our well-being as relationships with spouses and parents.[24] These connections shift over our lives, with the strongest connections to brothers and sisters tending to emerge in old age.[25] They may be particularly salient when we are confronted with difficult decisions about the care for aging or ill parents.[26] (See the box "Prioritize Extended Family Members.")

When Emma and Marcos Lopez decided to sit down and discuss their extended family, the conversation turned to their feelings of frustration with Marcos's parents. His parents seemed to reach out to Marcos only in a crisis or when they needed financial support. Marcos and Emma did their best to be helpful, but felt like they were giving

PRIORITIZE EXTENDED FAMILY MEMBERS

On your own, before you talk to your partner, think about the people in your extended family—your parents, siblings, cousins, and in-laws who are, or could be, part of the web of people who provide nurturance. How do these people fit into the vision you have for your family? How can you support one another in enacting your values?

Select a few of those relationships you'd like to enhance. But don't force it. Your short list will most likely include people with whom you have varying degrees of familiarity, and they may come from different generations, cultures, and backgrounds. The way you approach a conversation with your mother-in-law is likely to be different from your approach with your brother. By thinking in advance about how their lives can be enriched by more deeply connecting with you, you will be better able to tailor these conversations to the specific person and context in which you have them.

With your parenting partner (particularly when you're deliberating about your relationship with *their* parents or siblings), ponder what

more than they were getting back, and this was taking a toll on their lives as parents and on their work.

In talking about their relationship with Marcos's parents, they realized they had inadvertently distanced themselves from other people in Marcos's family, especially his sister, Fiol. They really only talked to Fiol when there was some new drama with their parents. Yet Fiol and her husband, Jack, live less than an hour away from them and have children about the same age. Emma and Marcos were curious about whether they might have a more substantial relationship with Fiol and Jack that didn't exist only to put out parental fires. They scheduled a you can do, individually and together, to enhance these relationships. Things to contemplate:

1. If you could let go of some of that old baggage, what would you want this relationship to look like?

2. Imagine seeing your relationship through their eyes. What do you think they care about most? What would they want your relationship to look like?

3. How might you change the way you engage with this person— as individuals, as partners, or as a family?

4. Is there a new way for this relationship to fit into the future you envision for your family?

5. How can you have this conversation in a way that is compelling, easy, and fun, given their personality and preferences?

6. Should you speak to this individual together or on your own?

family dinner and were able to have a meaningful conversation over dessert while the children played downstairs. As a foursome, they concluded that they could be proactive in creating the extended family that they all wished they had, rather than letting Marcos's parents dictate the terms of the family interactions. In reflecting on the conversation, Marcos said:

> I learned that they really value me as a positive male role model for their children. They see Emma and me teaching their children about the importance of family, love, trust, and fun. I had

TALK WITH YOUR VILLAGE

Having thought about all the friends, caregivers, community partners, and extended family members that are (or could become) a more meaningful part of your network, decide which of those relationships you'd like to focus on strengthening in the near term. It's not feasible to invest in all these relationships at once, either on your own, with your partner, or with your children. So, choose those relationships that have the potential to add the most value, joy, and love to your family, your career, and your sense of well-being.

Develop a simple plan together for how you can connect, with people or organizations, in light of all the things you've been discovering through this book's exercises. The main purpose, as ever, is to create greater mutual understanding. From that will flow more trust. Focus on the future, rather than on the past, letting them know why your relationship matters and asking about how you can strengthen it. Avoid making demands and just try to understand better what this person sees when they look at you and your future together.

never really thought about it, but the same goes for the time they spend with our children.

Another thing we discussed was the idea of family memories and traditions. We realized that Fiol and I can share family photos and stories with our children, rekindle some family traditions, and create new ones together. We came up with a few ideas for how we could celebrate Thanksgiving together, for starters. Emma and I want our children to have a sense of family and where they come from, so this idea was really exciting to us too.

Next, sit down and actually have these conversations with these people. Emojis sent via text messages won't do it. You want to convey that you are ready to invest in strengthening these relationships. Face-to-face (or via synchronous video) is much better. Ask questions, try to be vulnerable when it's relevant to do so, and express genuine curiosity about how they see things. Firming up these relationships requires a bit of conscious deliberation. Aim to clarify your common values, opportunities for mutual support, and the fit with who and what matters in the rest of your lives. Approach such conversations so all parties leave feeling better about the relationship.

Once you've had a couple of these conversations, reflect—both alone and with your parenting partner—on what you learned and any new ideas that might have popped up that you'd want to pursue because they might yield four-way wins.

As ever, record what you learned from the conversation as soon as you can afterward, so you hold on to the juiciest parts. In what ways do you now see your relationship or yourself differently? What insights or ideas emerged for ways that you might find greater harmony among the different aspects of your life?

In having this conversation with Fiol and Jack, Marcos and Emma realized they do not have to let their relationship be characterized by habits from the past; they have the power to move forward together to create family connections and traditions they did not get from their families of origin. And they feel more prepared to deal with Marcos's parents as a team the next time a problem rears its head. This readiness is a buffer that will protect against the strain of urgent demands from Marcos's parents and may also allow Marcos and Emma to be more attentive to their children and less distracted at work.

When our relationships with extended family members are working well, they can generate love for our children and support for us as parents. Yet old habits die hard, and we often get stuck in the assumptions we've brought with us from our childhood into adulthood. By making conscious, deliberate choices about how we join with our extended family, we have a better likelihood of avoiding destructive scripts from our past and discovering new forms of joy in this new phase of our lives together. (See the box "Talk with Your Village.")

With all of the writing and talking we've asked you to do, our hope is you're feeling more sanguine about your village and about the support its members provide you and your family. Now comes the real fun—undertaking experiments to create positive change. The goal: to make things better for people in all areas of your life so you can more fully and sustainably live your values together.

PART III

YOUR
EVOLUTION

Chapter 7

TRY A NEW WAY

Change needs to be made, and remade. It's the essence of what leaders do.[1] If you've been doing the suggested exercises so far—articulating your values and vision, talking with important people in your life, and thinking afresh about your future—you have likely noticed areas where your actions are at odds with your priorities as a parent and as a partner. Now you're ready to innovate: to try to create ways to meet the needs of the most important people in your world, to imagine how to make things better for them—and for you—and to bring them along with you as you lead toward that vision of a better future.[2]

Although Ryan and Leah Dettmer found it easy to blame one another for the challenges of co-parenting four young children, the Miami-based couple found it much easier to get on the same page when they started looking forward instead of backward. They started to explore ideas to help their family find greater harmony. Specifically, they wanted to emphasize acting responsibly and meeting commitments. So, they devised a chore chart. They wanted to teach their children to embrace their roles in the family. They also wanted to reduce their own housework, which was eating into downtime—time to talk with one another, and time to get enough sleep. This was especially true for Leah, who works part-time and is the primary caregiver. Ryan and Leah hypothesized that this experiment would be a win for all of them. Leah said:

I have had to choose between doing the housework while the kids are at school or both of us doing it after they go to bed. The potential benefits that could come from having the children take over some chores include being able to focus on work while the kids are at school, instead of feeling resentful that I have to do all of the chores myself. If we pack lunches and set out clothes in the evening, the children will be less frantic getting ready for school and there will be less conflict between Ryan and the kids to get out the door on time as he drops them at school. This will help us all feel less stressed and start the day on a better foot. The children will learn some new skills and see themselves as capable of helping out the family.

Sounds like a great plan, right? And it was. But after a few weeks, they saw flaws in the daily chore chart; the children's afternoon activities were pushing the tasks later and later into the evening, and there were no consequences for failing to do chores (or rewards for doing them). Some familiar patterns reared their ugly heads, too—Leah felt she was constantly nagging the children and was frustrated that Ryan didn't seem invested in progress. They were disappointed this experiment didn't work as they had hoped it would. But rather than thinking that the daily chore chart experiment had failed, they analyzed things and came up with a *weekly* chore chart that was more realistic. It still needed tweaking over time, but they were closer to finding a new way of doing things that enhanced all of their lives. When they reflected on this trial-and-error process, Ryan said: "I tend to want a methodical solution. I want to figure out what we should do differently and then just do it. I have a hard time accepting that we can learn from an experiment that doesn't work. I learned that you have to consistently step back, evaluate, and adjust. You're not going to check off a few things, and then voilà, it's finished. It's really never finished. And that's OK."

In this chapter, we'll guide you through the process of crafting experiments for how you live—and lead—your lives. You'll draw on all you've learned up to this point to generate ideas for new approaches that bring benefits to your home, your work, and beyond. These experiments will focus on achieving wins for your family and the other people in your lives, as well as for you.

But disrupting habits, familiar patterns, and longtime relationships can be daunting.[3] We'll focus on taking smart, *small* steps, which minimize the risks of change. Even within the limits of your everyday realities, you can move to a better place.[4] The goal is to produce sustainable changes. Adaptations will be more than just a flash in the pan because they make sense not only to you and your partnership, but to your children, to your work, and to your community. And, it's fun.

Think Like a Change Agent

An experiment is a planned change—something new that's a doable stretch.[5] It's a small step that builds competence *and* confidence. It is intended to have a positive and demonstrable impact. In the pages that follow, we'll invite you and your partner to come up with a couple of practical ideas for change—to act as change agents in your own lives.[6] We'll ask you to find age-appropriate ways of involving your children in your experiments so they can learn for themselves how to explore new ways of living joyful lives. You'll be modeling for them the skills all of us need to lead our lives, that is, to assume control and counter the natural tendency to just react to whatever comes along.

When people think of "experiments," they often picture a scientist in a laboratory with beakers and test tubes. That's not exactly what we mean when we say experiment, but it's a useful analogy. When you are designing experiments of your own, you are indeed a scientist in the laboratory of your life.

Experiments begin with a sense of wonder. They emerge from the question, "What if . . . ?" Experiments help us gain new knowledge and solve important problems. As you mull over the conversations you've undertaken so far with your parenting partner, children, and other key stakeholders, allow your curiosity to be piqued. Perhaps you've questioned some of your beliefs or habits in interacting with the people around you. Maybe you've noticed ways in which your actions don't square with what you really care about. It's likely you've had ideas about changes that might create a greater sense of control to feel peace in your lives while still achieving better results. Experiments provide a framework for using your imagination, pursuing your curiosity, and exploring how you might lead your lives differently—more fully alive—while serving those who depend on you.

But experiments bring uncertainty. While you'll be creating them in light of what you learned from conversations with people in your life, it's still impossible to know what will happen. Our research shows that it's the process of experimenting, more so than the outcomes of specific experiments, that really matters.[7] Framing your efforts as experiments releases you from the pressure to get things right, and you open yourself to the chance that some experiments might be more trouble than they're worth. The experimental mindset means this: the only failure from trying something new is the failure to learn from that experience.

By recognizing up front that leading change is a lifelong process, we accept that any one experiment may or may not be successful. We discover that each conscious step toward a vision reinforces our identity as a person willing to do things with purpose. As Ryan and Leah Dettmer learned with their chore chart concept, the experimental mindset can help you observe from a fresh perspective. The scientist isn't a failure if an experiment doesn't turn out as expected; surprises increase knowledge and make for continual learning. An important side benefit: if your children are old enough to notice, you'll be showing them the benefits of questioning the status quo and adopting a growth mindset.[8] And isn't that what we want for our children?

You don't have to overhaul your entire life to find greater fulfill-ment, individually or as a family. Any consciously designed change, if done with intention, can leave you feeling energized.[9] Just as scientific knowledge works incrementally, you can gain slight advances through each subsequent experiment. You do not need to change everything at once; in fact, that makes it harder to tell what's working. We've seen our fair share of ambitious experiments, from executives quitting high-profile careers and launching ventures to families selling their homes and taking a year to travel together. While we are inspired by these monumental changes, experiments work best when there is motiva-tion, access to resources, and extraordinarily strong social support. You don't have to upend your world to make meaningful and long-lasting changes. Actions as simple as taking family walks after dinner can show you the power of small wins.

Experiments begin with a hypothesis. If I change *this*, then I expect *that* will likely result. It is essential to define the effects that you want your experiments to have. These will vary, depending on how you, your children, or your partner are struggling and what precisely it is you want to alter, but the general principle is constant—the *intended ben-efit* is a four-way win: it is a change that results in gains at work, at home, in the community, and for our innermost selves. As parents, we are designing experiments that are wins for us individually, and for our children, our partner in parenting, and the other people we care about most. We call these *family four-way wins*.

You can't know the impact of a given experiment ahead of time. But the work you've done here has prepared you to develop well-informed hypotheses about what actions *might* yield family four-way wins. It might seem difficult to conceive of an experiment that has a positive impact for various people in multiple areas of life, but we've seen it hap-pen many times. You just have to give it some thought.

Rachel and Josh Steiner, who both work full-time in health care while raising Samuel, three years old, and Ethan, ten months old, decided to experiment with a date night every other week. "You always hear this idea that couples need to schedule time for date nights to keep the romance alive and blah, blah, blah," Rachel said. "It always just seemed like an unnecessary hassle since Josh and I watch TV together most evenings and we're together with the kids all weekend. We'd also have to find babysitters and deal with the kids being upset about our leaving."

When they came up with the idea of experimenting with date nights, Rachel and Josh didn't see how it connected to other aspects of their lives besides their relationship with each other. Yet when they reflected further, they realized they could have *double-date* nights—with other couples. In doing so, they could make more time for one another, and they could also strengthen their community of friends. They'd get a chance to eat some food other than the few kid-friendly meals on rotation at home. This would give them new sources of support about their work lives, too. They started to realize ripple effects—they would develop friends in their neighborhood that they could rely on, they would get their children used to having sitters, they would have adult conversations, and they would relax. Rachel and Josh experimented with this idea for two months and then reported back. Josh said: "Since we started this experiment, we went out three Saturday nights out of six. All three of the nights out were with other couples or friends. It allowed us to vent about our own lives as well as learn from our peers about things on their end. We have realized we are not alone in the struggle of raising little kids."

Double-date nights could indeed yield family four-way wins. Rachel and Josh benefited from the time they spent together as a couple, and their children got more comfortable with babysitters and gained some sense of independence and mastery. Spending time with their friends enhanced their feeling of connection with their community. The double-date nights also added fun and laughter to their life together, which provided a boost to their individual feelings of well-being. And they felt better able to handle work demands by truly restoring themselves.[10]

Pursue Family Four-Way Wins

Over two decades and thousands of Total Leadership experiments, we never cease to be amazed by the clever ideas that partners generate, frequently with the help of their children. We love telling the stories of the transformative experiments we've seen, but we do so with this caveat: do not feel constrained by the types of experiments we describe here. Think of them as launch pads. Come up with your own clever ways of leading of your lives together.

An essential feature of family four-way wins is that while the specific action taken in an experiment occurs primarily in one or two domains of life, it has intended benefits in *all* domains. Organizational psychologists call this "positive spillover."[11] A new exercise program with your spouse and children, for example, or even with friends and neighbors, produces greater energy at work and less impatience with your coworkers. The ideas in the next sections can be customized. They're not intended as rigid templates. Indeed, most successful family four-way wins are hybrids, or combinations, of the types we mention.

Generate Quality Time

A common theme among parents is that although they are spending time with the people who matter most, that time often lacks the attention, connection, and love that it merits. In your conversations, you may have heard a request from your children for your undivided attention. They want you to put away your phone. You may notice parallels elsewhere. At work, perhaps you're always reacting to emails but never getting to the projects that matter most. You may feel that you are going through the motions to get everything done, but the people you care about want more of you in your time together. Recognizing this pattern, many parents undertake experiments to create protected time, free from distractions and intrusions. Experiments that produce quality time can profoundly shift mindsets for busy parents who obsess about never having enough time because they're "crazy busy." Simply focusing on one thing can itself be calming.

One way that parents can create more quality time is to contain the digital deluge. Many of us with tween or teenage children assume it's our children who are addicted to technology, but when we step back and look dispassionately, we find the enemy is us: we can't curtail the nearly reflexive checking of work emails, news stories, or social media.[12] Some of the parents you've already met in this book chose to experiment with containing digital technology to allow themselves to be more present, in mind and not just in body.

Emma and Marcos Lopez embargoed technology in their bedroom. They expected that beyond the direct benefits to their relationship from reconnecting at the end of every day, there would be a benefit to their sleep. (Indeed, research shows that the light rays from screens interfere with sleep quality.[13]) Disconnecting from the outside world in the evenings might also reduce their stress levels. "It's probably not great for our health to get all riled up about the news and angrily scroll through Twitter right before bed," Marcos noted. Curtailing technology before bed could, they were betting, make them more energized in the mornings. They wagered they would greet their children in a better mood and arrive at work more alert.

Other quality-time experiments can involve the entire family more directly. For example, Leah and Ryan Dettmer decided to put aside their email and housework for a few hours to start family game nights on Saturday. In order to accommodate the six-year age gap among their children, they decided on a beanbag tossing game. They let the little kids stand closer and split up the stronger players to form teams. In looking back on this experiment, Ryan said this: "Surprisingly, there was minimal bickering. Whether it will achieve our broader goals of teaching them to be more cooperative remains to be seen, but I think if we continue to set aside Saturday evenings as sacred family time, we will find out."

Ryan and Leah also articulated the ripple effects of this experiment. Quality time together on Saturdays reduced guilt about their engrossed-in-work weekdays. Leah became more accepting of the weeknight hustle that sometimes felt more like chauffeuring than parenting. Shutting down work for a few hours on Saturday was at first quite difficult for Ryan, as president of a company, but he got used to assigning a VP to be on call for emergencies. Ryan and Leah also realized they could invite neighbors to play the beanbag game in their front yard. Now that the kids were able to cooperate and play nicely (most of the time), it didn't seem like a huge hurdle to add others to the mix.

Quality-time experiments are not just about being together with your family. Ravi Jain is a vice president of operations and father to Isha, fifteen, and Rishi, thirteen. Ravi and his wife, Anjuli, came up with a family four-way win in which the main action would involve Ravi spending time mentoring the younger members of the work team he leads. Using her expertise as a human resource manager, Anjuli helped Ravi design a plan to have a breakfast meeting every Friday morning with a different junior team member. While it meant leaving home earlier on Friday, and therefore required Anjuli to see the kids off to school, they believed that this experiment would yield positive change in all domains. Ravi said:

> This will allow me to proactively delegate, empower, and coach the younger team members. It will improve my sense of professional accomplishment by bettering me as a manager. It will also free me up to accomplish more important tasks on my main project at work, help me develop stronger relationships with these junior teammates, and perhaps help me delegate more to junior team members. If I am able to get some projects off my plate by

delegating, it will give me more time to spend at home with my wife and kids.

Quality-time experiments help us upend the wearisome premise that our problems are simply all about a lack of time. They compel us to choose what we do with the time we have. Our attention is perhaps our greatest resource as leaders.[14] Choosing to give our attention to the people who matter most—whether at work, at home, or in the community—increases the chance of spillover benefits, or ripple effects, in the various domains of our lives.

Let Go

We run into a lot of self-confessed perfectionists, people who are willing to invest whatever it takes to be successful in all the areas of their lives. While we try to help people redefine "success" and lessen the pressure to do everything perfectly, this can be hard to internalize. The notion that more success (as defined by living a life more closely aligned with your values) can sometimes mean working *less* is a tricky one to understand. It's worth experimenting with letting go of things you feel you *should* be doing but that, in light of your values and vision and the feedback from your key stakeholders, you should *not* be doing.

Lily Conrad, a project manager, and Brad Conrad, a web designer, decided early on that they both wanted to be engaged parents for their three-year-old daughter, Zainah. They were already quality-time champs. Brad calls himself the "social chairperson" in their relationship. During Zainah's few waking hours outside of daycare, Lily and Brad decided they would both be together, electronics off, focused on Zainah. While this shared, undivided attention hit high marks for quality time and made Lily and Brad feel like they were being good parents, it put pressure on them to get everything done outside of "Zainah time." Lily was leaving the office during her workday to run errands, and Brad was exercising after Zainah went to sleep. This wasn't working for them. Lily and Brad began to question and test their assumptions about how to be with Zainah.

As an experiment, they decided to take turns being the "lead parent."[15] While the lead parent spent focused time with Zainah, the other would do something else. Lily could work on her oil painting. Brad could jog on the treadmill while watching ESPN. Lily and Brad had to let go of the idea of being there for Zainah *at the same time*. But they figured that this would free up one parent, and it might be good for Zainah, too. She could get one-on-one time with each of them. It would also allow Lily and Brad to discover more about their individual parenting styles without the other judging, something that had become a source of tension. Plus, being freed up sometimes made each of them feel just a bit less stretched too thin. At first, they felt guilty, as though they weren't living up to their own definition of a good parent. But, after a few weeks of experimenting, they realized that they could find a new rhythm by letting go of archaic misconceptions.

Give some thought to where you might be overdelivering in order to live up to your own perhaps perfectionist, or simply untested or misguided, expectations and dictates. Whether it's how clean your house is, how nicely your reports are formatted, or how much you volunteer in your child's classroom, explore the possibility of letting certain things slide. If you're afraid your career will suffer, take heart in what our research reveals: when people reduce overall attention to work and focus more on high-priority tasks, while shifting some of their attention to other parts of their lives, they perform *better* at work.[16] Seems paradoxical—less time and attention devoted to work yielding better performance—right? Not when you realize that it's the result of working smarter and with less distraction.

And remember, these are just experiments. If you find you've relaxed a standard that was actually important, you can always go back to the old way of doing things. Or try another experiment.

Coordinate Logistics

Parenting requires complex coordination as well as communication skills to figure out who, what, when, where, and how to get things done. Operating in survival mode has many of us rigidly holding on to routines. Even something as straightforward as who folds the laundry—and exactly how those towels must be folded—might be so deeply embedded in our daily lives that we never think to question it. Yet, undertaking the exercises outlined here causes parents to question their habits. In many cases, they decide to try new ways to structure their days, communicate about logistics, or trade roles and responsibilities.

Sabra and Aryan Kabir, the Israeli expats living in Connecticut while Aryan grows his medical-supply startup, decided to create a family calendar to better coordinate their busy lives—Danya's swim team practices, Adar's karate lessons, Sabra's consulting commitments, and Aryan's business trips. Sabra and Aryan would input their own schedules and help their children add after-school activities, birthday parties, and other events. They would even schedule time to cook together on the weekends. Not only would this help them plan out each week, they surmised, it would teach their children computer and time-management skills. They anticipated that they'd all feel less stress if they didn't have to keep everyone's schedules straight in their heads, and they would avoid double-booking or forgetting about a sports practice. They hoped this experiment might also shed light on ways they might be overcommitting themselves and their children. Although they got off to a good start, religiously inputting their events into their shared calendar, they quickly fell off the wagon. The calendar became just another thing they had to keep track of and remember to do. In reflecting on this failed experiment, Aryan said: "The calendar was intended to help us manage the crazy number of different things we juggle. But maybe it's having all of those things going on that's really the problem. Sabra and I are going to try to simplify our weekday routines."

For other families, smarter coordination is about setting boundaries around the time and place that things get done. Zoe and Luke Bailey, for instance, decided that Luke would commit to being home by 5:30 p.m. for dinner twice per week. Up to this point, Luke, still new to his chief technology officer role, felt compelled to work long hours to prove his commitment. He relied on Zoe, who had stepped out of her teaching position when her kids were born, to manage dinner and the nighttime routine with their children. But she never knew in advance when to expect Luke. Luke had gotten into the routine of being the last person in the office, a choice he later acknowledged was driven by his subconscious need to feel as if he was making a contribution.

When Zoe and Luke reflected, they realized that they would have to live with Luke's long hours for a while. Yet they both wanted to find a way for Luke to be home for dinner with their children at least some of the time and for Zoe to have more predictability. So, they settled on the twice-a-week plan. Although Luke was primarily responsible for adjusting his work schedule, they felt shared ownership of this experiment. They were both committed to it. Luke said:

> I told my boss and colleagues about this experiment and enlisted their support in getting out the door by 5:15 p.m. on Thursdays and Fridays. They took the job of supporting me to heart. My boss would even remind me of the time if I was letting a meeting run too long. I felt like I had people at work who wanted me to be happy. Not only that, I felt like instead of being a role model for working ridiculous hours, I was now a role model for embracing the idea that we all have other parts of our lives that matter. A colleague even admitted that he felt more comfortable talking about his own family after he heard our boss remind me to get home on time one Friday. This is a needed change in our corporate culture. My taking the lead with this small initiative has been a net positive for my reputation in our company. And Zoe felt much calmer knowing she could put some plans into her

calendar, including going for a walk with her friend and attending parents' night at the school.

Practice Shared Values

Parents often notice a mismatch between what they say is important to them and what they practice in their everyday lives and cultivate in their children. If you found you listed important values in chapter 2 that are not being served in your daily life, think about what you might do to more fully embrace them as a family. This isn't about judging yourself for not focusing on them. It's also not about toppling your whole life to embrace an entirely new lifestyle. It's about finding small, creative, and fun ways to spend time doing things that are meaningful.

Choose something important and explore ways you might experiment to embody what you value. Joyce Casano and Anthony Aceto realized they wanted their children to learn persistence in the face of life's challenges. They certainly weren't planning to add real hardship to their children's lives, but they realized they could renew their children's swim lessons—a practice they had stopped because of all the whining and crying. Now that the children were a bit older and things were a little less hectic, Joyce and Anthony again signed up their children for Saturday morning swim lessons. Joyce had been a swimmer through high school and wanted her kids to fall in love with it. They could attend together as a family and make it into a challenge their children would, they hoped, eventually overcome. They decided to pair it with a family lunch together afterward. They even decided to talk to their kids about what they were trying to teach them about adversity and perseverance.

Joyce and Anthony saw other potential benefits of this family four-way win. As an elected judge, Anthony was building relationships and contributing to local activities, both things enhanced by the Saturdays out in the community. Having children who aren't afraid of the water would also open doors to spend more relaxed and fun time with family and friends at the beach.

Their second attempt at swim lessons was met with considerably less resistance, so it wasn't quite the lesson in grit that Joyce and Anthony had envisioned. But they felt very good about talking with their children about overcoming challenges, adding a fun and healthy activity to their lives, and having a great family brunch to look forward to each week—in addition to the bonus effects in their community, work, and personal lives.

Joyce and Anthony took a fairly abstract value (persisting in the face of obstacles) and linked it to a concrete experiment. Ideas for experiments are often more straightforward, requiring very little creative thinking. For instance, if you say you value your religion but rarely practice it, you might try attending religious services as a family. If you say you care about your health but never make it to the gym, you might explore ways to become more physically active. If you say you value your family of origin but rarely speak with your parents or siblings, you might schedule a regular contact. That's common sense, consciously considered.

This isn't just about adding another item to your schedule. It's about finding family four-way wins, looking at life from a new point of view wherein the seemingly disparate domains are all part of a whole. Even if it doesn't pan out the way you want, just thinking about the potential benefits in the different parts of your life builds your capacity to see more opportunities for harmony and peace in your lives together.

Build Health

Parents often experience a disconnect between the value they place on wellness and the attention they give to their physical and mental health. Caring for mind, body, and spirit has always been the most common Total Leadership experiment for parents and nonparents alike. For parents, though, it's more complicated because we are seeking *family* four-way wins. Any sustainable changes need to work in the often frantic reality of our interconnected lives. Yet, when you care for your own health, the attendant effects on your mood and energy level are likely to be felt by all of those in your immediate radius—your children, your coworkers, and others.

Almost every time we speak with a group of working parents, several will come up with the idea to simply wake up earlier and exercise before their children are awake. We hate to discourage people, but this experiment often fizzles out shortly after it's started. Parents usually overlook how this will actually be done *within the context of their lives*. It quickly begins to feel like just another unrealistic expectation. In caring for your health, think about how your experiment might create a scenario in which it is likely to feel the most invigorating, fun, and *manageable* for you *and* your family.

Camila and Peter Orlov, the retail executive and the investment banker, both recognized they were living sedentary lives, sitting in their cars and at their desks, despite the fact that Camila loves yoga and CrossFit, and Peter loves hiking and trail riding. They didn't want their young daughter, Charlotte, to see her parents ignore their health, and they did not want her to grow up ignoring her own. Peter and Camila decided to try a "pack walk" experiment: they would take an hour-long walk together with their dogs and daughter at least once every weekend. The reason they called it a "pack walk" was because dogs are pack animals, and, for them, the walk was a family connection: the Orlovs were the pack. This experiment was designed to allow Charlotte to participate in the experiment (albeit mostly from her stroller), give Peter and Camila some quality time together, check off a responsibility from their "must do" list (that is, walking the dog), *and* get them off their butts. Peter and Camila both anticipated that adding a little more activity to their lives would give them more energy throughout their workdays. They hoped that using the local trails and strolling through their town's main street might also help them meet some new people in their neighborhood and feel more connected to their community.

Peter and Camila reported that, after a few weeks, they were not only doing the pack walks every weekend, they were adding them on weeknights too. At five feet, Camila had to hustle to keep up with Peter's six-foot-two strides, but she didn't mind the added intensity. The pack walk created some unexpected outcomes, too. Peter realized that communing with nature was an important value that he had sidelined. Camila felt more connected with her dogs, who hadn't been receiving quite as much love since Charlotte's arrival. While an hour of walking might not seem profound for some people, for Camila and Peter, it was transformative.

Strengthen Networks

Despite providing ample research and testimonials about the importance of assembling a village, we encounter skeptical parents at every turn. Most parents feel they have no time to invest in building community. And we get it: you can't realistically join the parents organization at your children's school, volunteer at your house of worship, bond with your nanny, have a weekly mom's night out, and repair your messed-up relationship with your sibling all at once. But that doesn't mean you can't make intelligent investments in your community to yield family four-way wins.

Amy and Jack Brenner, the self-professed introverts and tech geeks, decided to go way outside their comfort zone and host summer outdoor movie nights in their Potomac backyard for neighborhood families. This experiment seemed ideal for many reasons, the first of which was that they realized they wouldn't have to clean their house for company if they hosted an outdoor event. It wouldn't cost them much money—they already had the projector, and a white sheet would work perfectly well as a screen. They could possibly make some friends. And they would engender some goodwill among neighbors whom they might be able to call on if they needed support. Their children might make friends they could play with on their block at a moment's notice, rather than relying on their parents to always schedule playdates in advance and shuttle them back and forth around town. Easier playdates could even free up some time for Amy and Jack to relax or take care of things around the house.

Six types of experiments for pursuing family four-way wins

Type	Description	Examples
Generating quality time	Create moments of quality attention and connection to make the most of time	• Having tech-free family dinners • Sponsoring one-on-one mentoring meetings • Kicking off family game nights
Letting go	Challenge perfectionism and reduce guilt to focus on what matters most	• Delegating weekly reports to a subordinate • Ordering a meal-delivery service instead of home cooking • *Not* volunteering to be the school room parent
Coordinating logistics	Plan new ways to get things done, seeking both efficiency and equality	• Putting dates on the calendar • Taking turns with pickup and drop-off • Coordinating work meetings and calendars with colleagues in advance
Practicing shared values	Emphasize values that haven't received attention commensurate with their importance	• Volunteering at an animal shelter • Developing a gratitude practice • Planning weekly family adventures
Building health	Take care of our bodies, minds, and souls to create energy, focus, and vitality	• Doing family Zumba at the gym • Setting earlier bedtimes for the entire family • Getting an annual mammogram
Strengthening networks	Foster connections to people and groups who can bolster us through life's trials	• Becoming a Girl Scout troop leader • Organizing a neighborhood potluck • Volunteering at the children's school

The experiment got off to a rocky start because of a thunderstorm, but they did manage to host a few movie nights over the summer. They put themselves out there and invited neighbors they hardly knew. After a while, it seemed they led the way toward a more engaged community of young families in their neighborhood; other neighbors took it upon themselves to organize barbeques and soccer games. Amy and Jack found the experiment to be extremely positive for themselves and their children. But they recognized that with the transition out of the summer months, they would need to design a new experiment that worked in lower temperatures, one that also didn't require them to make their house presentable. (For examples, see the table "Six types of experiments for pursuing family four-way wins." To begin yours, see the box, "Generate ideas for experiments.")

Collaborate in Creating Change

Your network of support can play a part in any changes you make. These people can help you think through how you design your plans for change, provide a reality check, hold you accountable, and get excited themselves about what you're doing because it may well benefit them. We've long recognized the power of support from others in the design and implementation of experiments. But this book takes this process one step further, because experiments will be something that you do together, primarily with your partner in parenting, but also with your children.

For those who do not have a co-parent, keep in mind that experimenting with a partner can be broadly defined. Crystal Zhang is a single mother with split custody of her two sons. She has a new boyfriend who has two children of his own, and she just started as vice president of sales at a Silicon Valley startup. She said that even though she shared custody of her children with her ex-spouse, she didn't feel that he was an emotional or intellectual parenting partner to her. When she thought about what an experiment partner might look like for her, Crystal recalled that when she took Stew's Total Leadership course during her Wharton MBA program, she and a classmate, Kiara, created an experiment together, becoming "meditation buddies."

Crystal didn't have children at that time, but when she revisited the idea of experimenting more than a decade later, she remembered her connection to Kiara and the transformative impact of meditating with a friend. Crystal decided to reach out to her again, asking Kiara whether

GENERATE IDEAS FOR EXPERIMENTS

The possibilities for experiments are endless. Now that you grasp the experimental mindset and have read about different types of experiments, let's design some. This process follows the pattern we've established throughout this book—start on your own and then work together with your partner. Like so much in our lives, experiments are better when done in collaboration.

Start by reflecting. Revisit the values you described in chapter 2. Have they changed as a result of what you've done since writing them? Which ones would you like to more fully realize in your daily life? Read the compelling picture of the future you created with your partner. What would it take for you to step closer? Look over your notes from conversations you've had with your partner, children, colleagues, and community members. Where do you see opportunities for greater harmony? How would the people around you benefit from your taking action to make things better for you and your family?

Write down ideas for things you could try that might lead to a family four-way win. The purpose of this exercise is just to generate new ideas, so don't worry if your ideas aren't worked out or even feasible. That part—refining your ideas and developing a plan for how you'll approach each of your experiments—comes next. Don't judge. Just imagine.

Push your ideas out of your head and compose them, whether in a notes file on your phone, on actual paper, as pictures, or in a light-hearted jingle. Remember, these might be actions taken by all of your family, some of your family, just you and your partner, just your partner, or just you. Let your creative juices flow and don't evaluate your ideas; get them down. Aim for five or six initial possibilities, knowing you'll be winnowing to two or three.

Your Initial Ideas for Family Four-Way Wins

Write a sentence that describes each experiment and another that indicates how you expect it would produce value for you and your family in all parts of your lives—your work, your home, your community, and yourself (mind, body, and spirit).

Your Best Ideas

Now, read over the list of experiment ideas you just generated. Consider the following in prioritizing your list of possibilities. Which of these ideas would be . . .

. . . easiest and most fun to do?

. . . most costly if you and your partner didn't do it?

. . . the richest opportunity for you and your partner to learn who you are and who you want to be?

. . . most likely to produce real benefits for you and your partner in all domains?

Select two or three ideas for experiments you would like to share with your partner for further exploration, experiments that are promising and exciting to you. Add to your description of each one any further thoughts about why you are enthused about it.

Share Your Experiment Ideas

With your partner, take turns describing the most promising ideas you generated on your own. Inquire about one another's ideas to improve your grasp, especially in terms of the potential for positive impact on all four domains of each of your lives. Then, as a partnership, answer these questions and write your responses:

(continued)

1. Are there any common themes across the experiments that you both shared?

2. Are there experiments that raise concerns or resistance for one or both of you?

3. Which experiments generate the most excitement or curiosity for you?

she was interested in rekindling the meditation buddy experiment, and was happy when Kiara enthusiastically agreed. They discussed how a return to meditation might have accompanying effects that spread throughout both of their lives and how rekindling their friendship would provide a valuable source of connection and joy in its own right.

Whatever your family structure, experiments should be jointly owned by the partners in parenting, not just one of you. This means that even if one of you is primarily responsible for making a change, the other partner still believes this experiment is going to result in family four-way wins, is actively involved in facilitating the experiment, and feels responsible for its pursuit. When you experiment together, it's about four-way wins for both partners, not just for one of you. You *both* have to feel as though you own the experiment: each of you has to be responsible for designing, implementing, tracking, and reflecting on and learning from your experiments.

In the case of Zoe and Luke Bailey, it was primarily Luke's responsibility to make sure he was able to get out of the office in time, but Zoe also felt bound to make this experiment work, so she shifted her morning routine for those days each week to help Luke get out the door earlier in the morning. Even when one partner takes the primary actions in an experiment, the other partner helps make it come alive. This could include emotional support, constructive accountability pressure, and encouragement. There may also be more concrete steps one partner can take to make it easier for the other partner, and these forms of support might not become apparent until the experiment is underway.

Children can play important roles in experiments, depending on their ages and capabilities. If it's developmentally appropriate, you can ask your children for suggestions on experiments you are planning. Of course, an experiment might be invisible to your children, even as they experience its benefits. For example, your children might have no idea that you've added a walk to your lunch break during work or have shifted which parent pays the bills. And yet, the reverberations we've discussed may have a noticeable effect on them. That's four-way thinking.

With practice, you will become more comfortable with being a family that experiments together. Your children will likely become more adept at shifting their perspectives and more open to trying things in new ways and demonstrating curiosity about what they discover. Depending on their capabilities, we recommend designing *at least one experiment* that directly involves your children. It should be exciting and fun, and have benefits for all family members, and even for others who matter in your life.

When Anjuli and Ravi Jain reflected on their values and vision, including the sustainability-focused startup they wrote about in their collective vision, they recognized that they didn't want to wait until they could quit their jobs in order to become more involved in giving back to their community and protecting the environment. Anjuli and Ravi, with their respective work responsibilities in HR and operations, had let their volunteerism fall by the wayside in the midst of their busy lives. Before having kids, they volunteered at the community garden, helped friends set up rain barrels, and donated to the Environmental Defense Fund. However, their kids were hardly even aware of their former enthusiasm for environmentalism. Meanwhile, their teenage

CREATE GAME PLANS AND SCORECARDS FOR YOUR EXPERIMENTS

Building on your conversations with your partner and children, decide with your partner which experiments are the most likely to generate *family four-way wins*. Write down which experiments you *both* agree are the two or three most promising. Hash it out until you *both* feel enthused about your choices.

Use the following template to think through how you'll approach these experiments. Start with a purpose statement for each experiment, and then write your responses to these prompts about things to keep in mind as you proceed.

Draft Your Game Plan

1. What is the purpose of this experiment?

2. What are you going to call this experiment?

3. What are you going to specifically do for this experiment?

4. How will this experiment yield family four-way wins?

5. How will you evaluate whether this experiment is succeeding?

6. What obstacles might you need to surmount?

7. What assets (strengths, resources, momentum) might propel your movement?

8. What do you expect to learn from this experiment, whether or not it succeeds?

The scorecard is intended to help you flesh out your responses to prompts four and five by pushing you to focus on different domains and relationships, one at a time. If you get stuck, try to think expansively about the spillover effects that a change in one aspect of your life might have on the others. For example, if you feel physically healthier, what might you do differently at work? If you connect with your children's caregivers or teachers, how might this help you be a more effective parent and coworker? If you are more engaged at work, how might you relate to your partner differently? The connections are there if you look for them, although they might not be obvious at first. By training your brain to see these interrelationships, you will be better prepared to take advantage of opportunities for family four-way wins now and in the future.

Fill Out Scorecards

Scorecards are used for tracking your progress toward goals. The table is a template for you to use in creating—in whatever form works best for you—a scorecard. Write the name of the experiment at the top and then take a few minutes to complete each cell.

Goals. For each experiment, describe the intended effect (that is, your hypothesis)—either the direct or indirect impact—you expect it to have on your *family* domain (separately on both your partnership and on your children) and then on each of your *career*, *community*, and *self* domains. Replace "Partner A" and "Partner B" with your actual names in the charts.

For community, if it makes more sense to think of your goal for this domain as the same for both of you, then simply replace "(Partner A)'s Community" with "Our Community" and ignore the row below that.

We urge you to leave no cell blank under "Goals." Even if you need to stretch your thinking, indicate some way this new action might have a positive impact on each of the domains. If the new action is just about your family, or your career, or your friends and community, or you, then it's not complete. It might be a great new thing in your life,

Experiment scorecard

Name of experiment: _____

Domain	Goal: Intended Impact	Metric: Measurement of Impact
Family: Our Partnership		
Family: Our Children		
Career: Partner A		
Career: Partner B		
Community: Partner A		
Community: Partner B		
Self: Partner A		
Self: Partner B		

but it doesn't pursue wins in all four domains—for both of you. And as wonderful as such a positive change might be, if it doesn't also include benefits in other domains, you're less likely to sustain it because there will be countervailing pressures, and lack of support, from the other spheres. Impact for your family and in all domains, for you and your partner—that must be the aspiration, even if you don't reach it. You're practicing the skills required to consciously, specifically account for the impact of the choices you make in all the facets of both of your lives.

Metrics. For each row, note what information you'll have access to that will indicate your progress, or lack of it. This data can be quite objective (for example, how many hours you work, how much you weigh, your children's grades in school, the number of outings you take together) or entirely subjective (for example, how you feel about your relationship, whether your work colleagues see you as having energy and empathy, or how spiritually alive you feel).

Get Moving

You're ready to go, so now it's time to make it happen:

- Start now by taking one small step in making the changes you planned.

- Talk regularly with your partner, your children, and any others who are involved as you move forward to find out what's working and what's not.

- Adjust continually as you discover new obstacles and new opportunities.

- Review your goals and track your metrics as often as seems reasonable, so you have data about how you're doing.

- Try to have some fun.

children, Isha and Rishi, were in a rather self-absorbed phase. Anjuli and Ravi figured they could reinforce for their children the value of helping those in need while reigniting this same value for themselves. They also saw that such an experiment could help them make new friends, contribute to their community, spend time together, and boost their children's college applications. They guessed it would also help them worry less about their children and thereby be less distracted at work.

Anjuli and Ravi held a family meeting to involve their teenagers in brainstorming about volunteer opportunities. All four family members did some more research on their own to identify organizations that needed help, taking into account their schedules, ages, and interests. They then shared ideas and decided on one volunteer option to select first: providing affection, care, and socialization to adoptable dogs and cats at the Humane Society. While Anjuli and Ravi had originally only considered the volunteering itself to be part of the experiment, they realized that involving their children in researching different volunteer opportunities was a useful change in and of itself. By tailoring involvement to a level that is appropriate for your children, you can help develop their self-efficacy—they will develop the confidence to make changes in their own lives. (To design your experiments, see the box "Create Game Plans and Scorecards for Your Experiments.")

We imagine you're itching to get started with making your experiments come alive, knowing the potential benefits they may yield. With a spirit of curiosity, and an acceptance that they will not likely go exactly as planned, go forth and experiment!

Chapter 8

SEE YOURSELF DIFFERENTLY

As you've done the exercises throughout this book, chances are you've noticed some changes in your life. You've grown in your capacity to lead in all areas of your life—by crafting a vision, undertaking courageous conversations, and exploring new ways of generating harmony and making life better. Now, after taking some time—weeks or perhaps months—to try a new way, you have an opportunity to make hay after all that tilling and sowing of your fields.

When Grace and Lee Yang started working with us, they were hoping for a little more clarity, peace, and fun in the midst of their demanding work schedules and the challenges of caring for their son, Adam, and managing his illness. They did not expect to have their lives radically transformed. They considered what they care about and who they want to be as a family and had conversations with those who matter most to them. Then they launched three experiments in pursuit of family four-way wins: a fundraiser for genetic research, having higher-quality conversations at dinner with Grace's parents who live with them, and finding ways for Lee's parents to connect with and care for Adam.

Six weeks after they began these experiments, we checked in with Lee and Grace. The first thing Lee and Grace proudly reported was that they had raised over $50,000 for research on Adam's genetic disorder. The add-on effects of this experiment and other activities were beyond what they had initially envisioned. Grace told us, "Now I am a catalyst for change. I do not need to sit on the sidelines while other people take charge." Lee said something similar: "I am not a victim of my life circumstances. I can pave the way to the future we aspire to instead of just letting it happen to me."

They reflected on how their relationship with each other had changed: "We've grown together as friends. We see a greater purpose for combining our talents to impact our broader community for good. We are able to nurture one another and communicate about how to work together to create the future we envisioned."

They wrote about how their relationship with Adam changed, too, saying while "he is still too young to understand what's going on, he will benefit if we feel empowered instead of victimized by his illness."

About work, they wrote:

> This process strengthened Grace's relationship with her boss by demonstrating her leadership skills, being more honest about her personal life, and learning to ask for support. Her organization donated funds and silent auction items, too. Lee realized that he cares deeply about work, but that he also needs to be more efficient and not let work consume his whole life. Lately, we've both done a good job managing work while striving to be faithful servants of God, great parents, and friends to our family and community. It's definitely still a work in progress, though, because it's easy to let work take over everything if we're not vigilant.

About their close friends, they wrote that sharing their story and asking for help strengthened relationships: "We learned that our friends actually want to be included in our 'real' lives, not just when things are going smoothly . . . They want to be there for us, and we've now learned how to let them. Our friends showed up en masse for the fundraiser."

About their extended families, they wrote: "We've improved our relationships with our families, too," adding that "conversations and experiments allowed us to understand others better, be more patient, establish healthier boundaries, and engage in ways that work for all of us. We've focused on making sure that we're treating them as part of our family, not just caregivers."

In their community, Grace and Lee said that they see themselves as leaders and advocates and feel they can help others affected by Adam's disease. "It's helped us see the bigger picture beyond our own lives."

The future looks different to Grace and Lee Yang. They're on a new path together as a team, as parents who lead.

An essential part of the work before you now is to reflect on your exploits. Take a moment to think back on how things are different—or not—from the way they were when you started. If you haven't yet had a chance to try an experiment or two, then bookmark this page and come back to it.

Try revisiting the four-way view table we introduced in chapter 3. Ken and Ashley Hubbard, who were seeking ways to build community in Montreal while Ken completes his MBA, completed their "after" four-way view chart a few months after their "before" chart. They noticed some significant shifts in the ways they saw themselves and their lives as parents of their one-year-old, Ava.

Their before and after scores are in the table "Changes in Ken's and Ashley's four-way views."

Ashley and Ken didn't dramatically overhaul what they viewed as important or make huge shifts in where they focus their attention. Yet they reported increased satisfaction in *all* areas of their lives. Ashley and Ken are fairly representative of the parenting partnerships we've been studying. Following small, smart, intentional shifts in attention, parents generally report increased satisfaction with the different facets

Changes in Ken's and Ashley's four-way views

	Importance before	Importance after	Attention before	Attention after	Satisfaction before (1–10)	Satisfaction after (1–10)
Ken's changes						
Career	45%	40%	45%	40%	6	7
Family	35%	40%	40%	40%	6	9
Community	5%	10%	5%	10%	4	6
Self	15%	10%	10%	10%	3	7
Ashley's changes						
Career	30%	25%	40%	30%	4	8
Family	50%	50%	45%	45%	4	8
Community	10%	15%	10%	15%	5	7
Self	10%	10%	5%	10%	3	6

of their lives.[1] Most importantly, these different facets can improve *at the same time*. This stands in contrast to the assumption many parents hold when we start working with them, that to improve one area of your life, you have to make sacrifices in another.

It doesn't always have to be a zero-sum game. Family four-way wins *are* possible, and you don't have to completely revamp your life to achieve them. Adjusting how you look at your life, how you invest your most precious resource—your attention—and how you engage with those around you can be more powerful than you ever dreamed. (See the box "Take the Four-Way View Now.")

Having done some experiments together over a couple of months, Deena Altman and Jake Center each described how their perceptions of their lives have shifted. Deena said:

> This process prompted Jake and me to talk about some things we were both thinking but hadn't yet formally discussed. Jake has a better understanding of some of the fears and concerns I have as a working mother and guilt that I may not be doing a quality job in that role. Now, Jake is more focused on tech-free family time, being with me, and being present. Before, he was often distracted by his phone. My hope moving forward is that Jake sees value in other experiments in our roles as parents, spouses, and employees and that he recognizes he has the power to change a situation if he's not content with it.

Jake said:

> I think Deena got much more comfortable communicating with me regarding what she needs and expects from me, not just about our relationship, but in terms of family and time for herself. This flows more organically now rather than our having to set aside time to talk about it intentionally.

TAKE THE FOUR-WAY VIEW NOW

Take another crack at your four-way view tables from chapter 3, both yours and your partner's. Completing them again gives you information that can enrich your understanding of what you've learned from your experiences in articulating what matters, connecting with the people who matter, and trying new ways of generating family four-way wins.

Your Four-Way View Now

As you complete your four-way view now, please do so *without sneaking a peek* at what you wrote back in the beginning, not, that is, until you complete the accompanying tables according to how you see things today.

The second column asks you how important each of the four domains is to you. These numbers should add up to 100 percent. For the third column, think about how much attention you actually focus on each domain in a typical week or a typical month. Assign a percentage to each domain to represent the fraction of your attention that you devote to each domain and be sure that these numbers also add up to another 100 percent. In the last column, rate how satisfied you are with each domain on a scale of 1 to 10, with 1 meaning "not at all satisfied" and 10 meaning "fully satisfied." Please complete the table about yourself now.

My four-way view now

Domain	Importance	Attention	Satisfaction (1–10)
Career	%	%	
Family	%	%	
Community	%	%	
Self	%	%	
	100%	100%	

Now look back at how you completed this table the first time. Compare your responses with what you just wrote and think through these questions:

1. How is your life different now? Where are the biggest changes and what has remained pretty much the same?

2. Beyond the numerical changes, in what ways has your approach to life changed?

3. What further changes do you now want to make moving forward?

As ever, it's helpful to jot down some notes in response to these questions. This will enhance the value of the conversations you have with your partner, coaches, and perhaps others about what you have discovered.

Your Partner's Four-Way View Now

When we asked you to take the four-way view of your own life in chapter 3, we also asked you to contemplate your partner in parenting—how they engage with the different aspects of life, manage attention, and feel about how things are going in each domain. By reflecting once again on your partner, you can help them see changes not otherwise recognized or aspects of life that have remained the same. These insights are crucial to building your capacity to lead together from here on.

Consider the changes you've noticed in your partner over the past several months and complete the four-way view for your partner as you see them now. This isn't about pinpoint accuracy. As we said the first time, make every effort to provide your best, albeit subjective, assessment of your partner. From your perspective, how

(continued)

important is each domain and how much attention does your partner pay to each domain? How satisfied do you think your partner is (from 1 to 10, with 1 meaning "not at all satisfied" and 10, "fully satisfied")?

Please complete the table about your partner now.

My partner's four-way view now

Domain	Importance	Attention	Satisfaction (1–10)
Career	%	%	
Family	%	%	
Community	%	%	
Self	%	%	
	100%	100%	

Think about these numbers and what they say about how they have changed over the last weeks and months you've been exploring and experimenting together. How has your partner changed, if at all? How would you describe your partner now? Take a few minutes to reflect on and write a few notes about these questions:

1. How, if at all, has your partner changed?

2. What is the greatest hope you have for your partner from this point forward?

3. What do you most appreciate about what they have done in your work on the exercises in this book?

Then talk over your responses with your partner.

I hope Deena sees herself as the amazing mother and wife that she is. She has always been very career-oriented and ambitious, and maybe she did not feel like she was putting enough focus on our relationship or our home life. But I think she does a tremendous job, and I want her to recognize that the boys and I see this.

I appreciate that Deena has done her best to keep me on track with my engagement in this process, not only by active measures, but also by being receptive to my thoughts and feelings in our conversations and by having a positive attitude, making it easier for me to view these exercises as something we enjoy doing together.

By seeing one another more clearly and supporting one another in their goals, Jake and Deena strengthened the foundation upon which they are building their lives together.

Grow as a Family

If there's one thing we can say with great confidence after years of facilitating experiments designed to produce four-way wins, it's that the *process* of experimenting is *more important* than the specific experiments themselves.[2] A central goal of our approach is to help you become a family that experiments intelligently—together, with purpose and with passion. Reflecting on your experience is essential in order to crystallize what you've learned about how to design sustainable change, how to muster the will to try new ways of doing things, and how to become increasingly competent as a family propelling yourselves into the future. What worked well, what did not, and what did you discover about striving to make positive change?

Lisa Davis and Eddie McDonnell, in addition to a "hike and pick" experiment, in which they picked up trash while going for a family walk, also did an "Eddie comes home for dinner" experiment, in which Eddie was going to come home from work in time for everyone to eat together. The hike and pick experiment went pretty much according to plan—the family four-way wins they hoped for materialized. They were getting exercise, spending more time together, giving back to their community, and on occasion, bringing their coworkers along for the walks, too. Lisa and Eddie were ready to embed their walks together into their ongoing family routines.

The plan for their second experiment was that Eddie would get home for dinner by 7:30 p.m. on weeknights. This experiment also had well-intended family four-way wins—Lisa and Eddie would more evenly share evening responsibilities, Eddie and the children would have more quality time together, Lisa would have greater flexibility to attend after-work gatherings, update her Etsy shop, and join the PTA. For Eddie, coming home for dinner was expected to improve his performance at work by forcing him to prioritize, increase his focus, and be more efficient.

The experiment started out strong, with Eddie getting home from work in time for dinner most days. Lisa felt less stressed throughout her workday and into the evenings knowing that the evening routine wasn't on her shoulders alone. She signed up for the PTA, too. But over the next few weeks, two things happened. First, Eddie started to arrive home later and later. Although he was making it home for bedtime much more consistently than before, he was no longer making it home by 7:30 p.m. Second, Eddie was falling behind on client and management expectations. Simply put, his performance at work was suffering. "I can't keep this up if it means I'm going to fall behind on important projects and let my clients and bosses down," Eddie said.

While Lisa wasn't oblivious to the fact that Eddie's work hours started to creep later and later, she didn't realize how much he felt as if his work was suffering and the stress it was causing him. Lisa said: "Eddie wasn't complaining, so until we went through this process of reflecting on the experiment, I didn't realize how much angst he was feeling about his work. Our children and I want to spend more time with Eddie and have him help out around the house, but if it's adding a ton of stress or causing problems at his job, it's not worth it."

Despite the several ways in which the experiment benefited different facets of their lives together, it wasn't turning out to be a family four-way win. Rather than feeling as if their experiment was a failure, though, Lisa and Eddie were able to reframe it and thereby learn something important from it. Eddie said:

> This experiment showed me that I can't just put a Band-Aid on the fact that my workload exceeds what one person can reasonably do. Over the last few years, I've taken on more and more responsibilities without ever taking anything off of my plate. If I want things to change, I realize I'm going to have to have some more in-depth conversations with my senior manager and team to rethink how we do our work. It's looking more and more like our next experiment will involve me initiating some of these conversations at work.

For Lisa and Eddie, the experiment revealed an underlying barrier to creating the harmony they both desired. Eddie is in the fortunate position where he can initiate conversations about these hurdles without being afraid that he will lose his job. In fact, it might demonstrate his leadership skills. Not everyone is in such a position— sometimes rocking the boat is just too risky. But there is still value in finding what works for you, within the realities of your own lives, and seeing the real obstacles in the way of your having more harmony and calm. Experiments that don't go according to plan often expose hidden assumptions and reveal unforeseen paths toward making positive change. Realizing this can feel good, as it did for Lisa and for Eddie.

REFLECT ON YOUR EXPERIMENTS

Some of the most long-lasting insights come from experiments that failed or that were altered significantly as a result of the implementation. *The only failure here is the failure to learn from what you tried to change.* The next set of questions asks you to look back at what's transpired, to see what you've learned. Then it asks you to look forward to your future together through a new, clearer lens.

Write down what happened in each of your experiments and the results. Look back at what you indicated in the last chapter about the expected benefits you anticipated from each experiment and the goals you hoped to achieve. Then, for each experiment, describe what actually happened. For each experiment, ask yourselves:

1. What actually happened? Did you do the experiment as you originally designed it? Did you abandon or adjust your experiment?

2. Overall, on a scale of 1 (complete failure) to 10 (goals and results fully achieved), how do you rate this experiment?

3. How did the experiment affect the different facets of your lives, individually and together? In what ways, if at all, did this experiment change your relationship and relationships with your children; your work performance and motivation; your connections with friends, extended family, and broader community; and your minds, bodies, and spirits?

4. Does this experiment inform how you want to lead your lives moving forward? What do you want to keep doing, stop doing, or do differently?

Taking time to reflect on our experiments allows us to see ourselves as partnerships capable of creating change. Over time, as we experiment together, our confidence grows and, with it, our willingness to try new ways of living our lives. We start to notice latent opportunities for greater alignment. Experimenting together builds a shared language and gives us tools for approaching life together, seeing more opportunities for shaping the future. (See the box "Reflect on Your Experiments.")

Teach Each Other

Our approach to learning how to be a parent who leads isn't about finding specific ways to get through the daily hassles. While you may find some useful life hacks within these pages, this book is about more than tips for the everyday. It's about seeing ourselves as leaders capable of creating lives driven by values and purpose, for ourselves, our children, our world: it's about having a code—as Crosby, Stills, Nash & Young famously sang—that you can live by.[3]

As parents, we are raising the next generation. At a time when our world seems ever more overwhelming, divided, and fragile, we can raise children who seek peace, harmony, justice, and who care for the earth.[4] As one parent put it, "The kids notice. They notice every action, every experiment. They are listening and watching us. And we can choose what we're teaching them about themselves and the world through our words and actions."

In chapter 4, we described the main things our children need from us as parents: safety and security, attention and affection, values and morals, and clear expectations. Our purpose then was to push you to question what your children really want and need from you. You might have come to realize, for example, that the quantity of time you spend with your children is not the sole metric of the quality of your parenting. Beyond that, we offered that simple classification as a guide to help you think about the unique needs of your children, in whatever phase of life they're in right now.

In the process of talking with and experimenting with your children, you may have shifted some of your impressions of them. Amy and Jack Brenner learned that their children, now transitioning into the tween and teen years (at ages eight and thirteen), are more perceptive than they had realized. Amy said:

> We learned they are much more thoughtful than we gave them credit for. In some ways, they are way ahead of us . . . they're not as stuck in their habits as we are. Right now, they are so honest, creative, and fearless. We want to give them the skills and strength to stay that way as they become young adults. Our next experiment will be to create regular activities that allow us to practice these things as a family so we don't lose the momentum that we've created.

Peter and Camila Orlov, on the other hand, have a toddler and another baby on the way. Although they didn't initially design an experiment related to bedtime, they ended up creating an impromptu experiment. Initially, their guilt about not spending enough time with Charlotte led them to provide endless stories, lullabies, cuddles, and kisses at bedtime. The bedtime routine would drag on for hours, and despite how much they cherished those affectionate hours, the routine was taking a toll. They assumed that when their daughter was asking for "one more song" at bedtime, she was telling them what she needed. Despite talk of sleep training, it never felt right to forgo affection when it was so clearly desired.

In a moment of insight (that seemed obvious in hindsight), Camila wondered whether perhaps Charlotte didn't actually know what she needed from her parents. Then and there, Camila and Peter started an experiment with the bedtime routine. They told her that they would have fifteen minutes for cuddles and stories and that they expected her to stay in bed quietly after that point. They reassured her that they would be nearby and that she was safe. Peter said:

> I thought we would have a massive meltdown and be up all night listening to her cry. To our surprise, she just looked up at us and said, "OK." I won't pretend that every night thereafter went quite as smoothly, but we drastically cut down the time we spent putting her to bed each night. She's getting better rest, and we've gotten some time in the evenings to be together and relax. Before that night, we were letting our guilt drive our bedtime routine. Moving forward, we don't want to let our parenting decisions be dictated by our guilt or by the demands of a two-year-old. And, with another one on the way, we realize that we need to be proactive in keeping this process going.

Whether you're like Amy and Jack Brenner, who realized that their children had more insight than they knew, or like Peter and Camila Orlov, who realized that children can't always differentiate needs from wants, allowing yourselves to see your children in a new way and to involve them in the process of experimenting with you can have a lasting impact on all of your lives.

Welcome Surprises

We started this book by acknowledging how challenging the parenting journey can be as you strive to nourish your children, grow your careers, strengthen your relationships, and engage as citizens. We want to end in the same way—by acknowledging that no book can make this journey easy. All of us continue to struggle, lose sight of the bigger picture, and feel pulled in many directions. We believe that even the struggles can be empowering. Your story is unfolding. You now have some tools you can use again and again, with increasing facility, as your children grow, your career aspirations shift, your relationship deepens, and your network of love expands. The exercises stay constant, but the experience of doing them is constantly evolving, as are you.

This process is deeply personal. Other than our recommendation to get enough sleep and avoid corporal punishment, we've stayed far away from prescriptive advice about how you *should* lead your lives. The values that unite you, the vision that inspires you, the relationships that nurture you, and the habits that drive you are unique to your family. Yet you are not alone. You are part of a community of parents striving to find a better way, continually learning more about what it means to lead together.

Here are some reminders we hope you find useful. We, Alyssa and Stew, refer to them regularly in our lives, especially during the hard times, because they help us to keep our eyes on the prize—meaningful lives, lived together.

You Have More Love and Support in Your Life Than You Realize

So many parents feel they are struggling alone. It's not uncommon for parents in our workshops to lament that they no longer have "villages" to help raise their children but think that building their own community would take too much time, until experiments show them that it isn't so time-consuming after all. We shared the story of Lee and Grace Yang, who felt isolated by their child's illness yet learned that when they were vulnerable and asked for help, it was abundant. Many parents don't realize that their friends are struggling, too, until they reach out to form a coaching exchange and find other couples with whom they can share experiences. When the chaos of daily life drives you inward, it's useful to keep in mind that when you seek out support, cultivate it, and give it back to others, you usually find you are much less alone than you had thought.

You Don't Know Your Partner as Well as You Think You Do

So far, we haven't worked with any parents who revealed dramatic secrets or hidden identities. Yet many of the parents in our programs operate on the assumption that they know what's going on in the head of the other at all times.[5] That's not surprising, given that some partners have been together for decades. But when we proceed as if this assumption is true, we run the risk of putting our relationship on autopilot. Complacency turns into habits, which in turn limit creativity and exploration. When partners actually talk about what matters most to them and how they want to live their lives, alone and together, new doors open up for meaningful change.

We told you about Lily and Brad Conrad, who uncovered an important discrepancy between how Lily was actually spending her time (doing family-related errands and tasks during her work hours) and how Brad perceived it. Once they were able to be honest about what they're actually thinking and doing, they were able to work toward a more accurate understanding of each other's experiences and collaborate to find solutions that work for both of them.

The Expectations You Place on Yourself Aren't Always Real

We tell ourselves a lot of stories about how good employees, parents, partners, and so on are supposed to act. And, we behave as if these stories are true. We encouraged you to question those assumptions by talking with the people who matter most to you. Deena Altman described to us how she always felt guilty, as though she could never live up to the expectations that people had of her. Yet, when she finally began to check the reality of those expectations, she learned that they didn't hold her to the same standard of perfection she pushed herself to achieve. "This realization gave me the freedom to not be so hard on myself," she said, "and to make choices that are driven by what I actually care about instead of my fear of letting people down."

You Have More Freedom to Make Changes Than You Think

We often hear parents say that it's *impossible* to change certain features of their lives. We live in the real world where some things truly might not be changeable—like a project due date, school start time, or length of your commute. Yet, many parents are surprised by how many things in their lives actually *are* malleable. Remember Luke Bailey, who realized he could leave the office earlier a few days a week once he got his team and boss on board, and Joyce Casano, who started working from home on Wednesdays. These changes can be dramatic. When parents feel trapped by the conditions of their lives, they are often surprised to learn that simply asking the question, "Can this be changed?" is incredibly useful, even if the answer is sometimes no. The realization that our lives are more tractable than we thought is an empowering shift.

Small Changes Can Generate Big Wins

By the time parents come to us, they're often so overwhelmed with the demands of work, family, and the rest of life that they believe the only way to fix things is through a massive overhaul. And, sometimes a massive overhaul is exactly what's needed. But, before you quit your job, take heart in the knowledge that most of the parents we encounter are delightfully surprised at the big impact of small changes, intentionally made. Thoughtfully designed experiments can generate four-way wins that shift how you feel about your lives without radically changing how you live them, as we saw in comparing the two sets of Ken and Ashley's four-way views. Even small initiatives like a chore chart, a hike and pick, or a weekly mentoring meeting can have positive cascading effects throughout the different aspects of your lives.

You Are a Leader

A shift that surprises many of the parents in our workshops is the realization that they are indeed leaders, that is, they are people capable of mobilizing others toward a goal that matters. Whether they are in a formal leadership role or not, they realize they have the capacity to inspire others. Rather than seeing themselves as managers who oversee to-do lists and make sure things get done, they start to view themselves as leaders who set a vision for the future and bring others along with them. With the support of her husband, Marcos, Emma Lopez became aware of how she could change the culture of her workplace by modeling the importance of attending to life outside work. Each of us, in our own way, alone and in concert with our partners, has the power to breathe new life into the world with a vision of a better future. We can help the people around us move toward it with us. (See the box "Harvest the Fruits.")

None of this is written in stone, of course. Your priorities will likely evolve over time. You might want to put a reminder in your calendar to reread them a month from now, both to see if any new insights emerge in the upcoming weeks and to make a habit of talking about them. Why not just add a quarterly recurring reminder to check in on what matters most in your lives together?

As you move down the road together, don't just revisit these surprises. Find new ones and share them with others in your world. Be a parent who leads.

HARVEST THE FRUITS

The most important part of any learning process comes at the end of a cycle. This is a time to harvest the fruits of your labor and to expand your capacity. These last few questions are intended to help you to do just that. First, on your own, separately, write a few notes in response to these questions:

1. What surprises occurred to you as a result of your work on the exercises in this book?

2. Reread the shared values and collective vision you created in chapter 2. Edit what you wrote together according to how you see things now.

3. In reflecting on any changes you observed in yourself, your partner in parenting, and your children, how can you use what you've learned as you move forward as a family that experiments together?

Then, one more time, share your responses to these questions with your partner. Talk with them about what you will do to honor the joint commitment you've made for the future you're designing. How will you build on the insights you've gained and the momentum you've generated so far?

Postscript

SPEAK OUT

We hope you now see that you have more freedom to lead the life you want as a parent than you might have thought. Yet we exist in a society that creates enormous hurdles for working parents. While the focus of this book is on how and what you can change in your life and in your lives together, it's important to remember that the challenges you face aren't simply a matter of you not trying hard enough or being creative enough.

There are cultural and structural barriers that make it difficult for parents to be meaningfully engaged in their careers and their family lives, particularly in the United States. This book wasn't intended to address those broader societal changes needed to support working families. We focused on what *you* can do in the upcoming months and years to make things better in your immediate world.

But our vision is to change the world for the better—to help working parents feel empowered and fulfilled as they strive to raise compassionate and engaged citizens. And, if we have to, we'll do that one family at a time. Indeed, that's why we wrote this book. One family at a time can feel, however, like an awfully slow way to move mountains. Sweeping societal changes—like universal paid family leave, a living wage, affordable childcare, universal pre-K, portable health care that does not handcuff you to a job that isn't otherwise viable, and closing the gender pay gap—will accelerate our movement toward a more just world for parents, particularly for the most vulnerable and disenfranchised members of our society.

If you want to help pursue this vision, add your voice to the choir raising its voices about the social changes we need to support working parents. Advocate on behalf of those who are struggling for survival, who do not have the resources that you have to improve their lives. Vote for political candidates who prioritize the needs of working parents. Do what you can to ensure your company's policies for parents apply to workers at all levels, for fathers as well as mothers, and for those adopting and fostering children. Speak out to give voice to those who are not heard.

You have the tools to realize a better future. Examine your collective vision and, if need be, add something about what you want your legacy to be in making the world better for other parents and their children. Design an experiment that embraces such advocacy. Most of all, inspire others to join you on this journey by helping them see—as we've tried to in this book—how they benefit, how we all benefit, when all parents feel themselves to be leaders.

Appendix

BUILD A COACHING EXCHANGE

Being a parent who leads is among the most significant aspects of your life. And it can be even more fruitful when you have others helping you through the ups and downs. In our work with parents, we've found that a key element in the creation of lasting, positive change—of learning how to lead together with love and also with a passion—is the support of other parents, of fellow travelers. In our workshops, we create "coaching exchanges," matching parenting partnerships with others to exchange writings, provide feedback, maintain accountability, and swap ideas. This does not mean that you and your partner need to divulge intimate details of your relationship that you don't want to reveal to others, but it does mean that if you are willing to talk about your experiences, you can get some unbiased input. When these exchanges work, you may choose to stay in touch with your fellow coaches long after going through the complete process, staying updated on new developments and even doing booster sessions to inoculate you against regressing into old habits when needed.

Give and Receive Coaching to Improve Performance

We have urged you throughout this book to share the various elements of this experience with your parenting partner and to coach each other by asking clarifying questions, pushing for deeper understandings, and cheering each other. But there are real benefits to reaching beyond your most intimate relationship for coaching, pair to pair. First, when lives get hectic, partners in parenting find it easy to let the exercises in this book fall to the bottom of the to-do list; a coaching exchange can help you stay on track. Also, when you and your parenting partner are in the thick of raising children and pursuing your careers—while trying to take care of yourselves *and* have some other meaningful connections to people—it may seem as if you are the only ones sweating it out. But when you talk to others who face these same challenges, you learn you're not alone. Parents report to us that simply hearing about the stories of other working parents provides encouragement, fresh perspectives, and new ideas for action. "I feel better about myself knowing that it's not just me that's struggling with how to make everything fit together," said Jack Brenner, the Potomac-based introvert who, along with his similarly quiet wife, Amy, experimented with strengthening their connections to colleagues, friends, and neighbors. "No one's got it all figured out and we're all trying to find better ways. It's energizing to be part of that."

Further, you and your parenting partner have developed habits of doing things in the same way. Engaging in a coaching exchange can help you see things from a different vantage point. And when you coach others, you get novel ideas about your own leadership, in your work and in your life beyond work, while giving support to someone else.

We know that not everyone who picks up this book will have someone they consider a true partner. If you are a single parent, or (either by choice or by circumstance) don't have a partner who is involved as a parent, reaching out to create a coaching exchange can offer camaraderie. You may find that a coaching exchange offers rich resources beyond just parenting.

But there's vulnerability that comes with inviting another person or couple to join you on this journey. Not only are you asking them to commit time to reading this book and energy to doing the exercises, you're asking them to read about your personal values, dreams, and relationships. In return, you'll offer to hold them accountable and share your own reflections based on what you read in their exercises. Remember, you don't ever have to reveal more than is comfortable. We'll do our best to help you identify and establish coaching exchanges (visit www.ParentsWhoLead.net for more information). And we encourage you to be proactive in connecting with others.

We're not suggesting that you become a professional coach. This appendix offers pointers to help you and your friends, colleagues, and family members use some basic coaching concepts to enhance your experience of completing these exercises together. But your coaching exchange is not a replacement for professional coaching or counseling support, which you should seek when problems in your life reach a crisis point, or when your current resources just aren't sufficient.

Launch a Coaching Exchange

To create a coaching exchange, start by thinking about parents in your personal and professional networks. Approach those with whom you'd like to collaborate. Potential coaching partners might be coworkers, friends, members of your community or family—anyone who is interested in going through the Parents Who Lead journey with you. You may find it most useful to form coaching exchanges with parents who have children in a similar age range as your own, though there is still much to be gained even if the ages of your children vary.

Once you have identified an interested potential coaching partnership, find a time for the four of you to chat about your goals. Coaching partnerships have accomplished this in different ways, including meeting for an adult-only meal, chatting via video call after children are in bed, and setting aside time to speak on the phone on a weekend afternoon when children are otherwise engaged. Each member of the group should be able to devote full attention to the conversation.

To get the most out of this initial conversation, both partnerships should have their own copy of the book and should have read chapter 1 and responded to the questions it asks about goals, both individually and as a partnership. Focus like a laser on goals for the coaching experience. A primary purpose of this first meeting is to clarify expectations for the coaching exchange. Expressing your goals increases the likelihood of obtaining them. The more open you are about what you want to gain, the more likely you will be to realize those aspirations, because your commitment will be higher and because people will know how to help you. In this first conversation, discuss what you're most looking forward to and what you most dread. Try not to hold back.

This is also a good time to talk about how you hope your coaching exchange will work. Set times to meet and discuss how you'll share written responses to the exercises in the book. Parents have found it useful to share their exercises electronically at first and then read and comment on those responses before meeting to talk about them. Each member of the group needs to be committed. The value and quality of the actual conversation about the material are enhanced when *each* member of a coaching exchange has digested other members' responses. Again, only make public what you are comfortable exposing with your coaching partners but push yourself to develop a deep level of trust by being as open as you can.

In your coaching partnership, you'll have a chance to be both coach and client (the term we prefer to describe the person receiving input from coaches), and you and your parenting partner stand to benefit from both roles. We recommend you take turns acting as coach and client, with one coach and one client pair at a time. To get value from coaching, a client's main challenges are to remain open and to contain defensive reactions to feedback. This can be difficult because our natural tendency is to justify our actions. Do your best to adopt a spirit of inquiry, keeping in mind that the goal is gaining new perspectives. If you hear a question or comment that makes you a bit uncomfortable, greet it with curiosity—as a kind of gift, even—and strive to respond with candor.

A coach's responsibility is to gain an understanding of the client's key relationships at work, at home, and in the community, while identifying strengths and areas for improvement. This boils down to asking questions about whatever strikes your interest or seems unclear as you read the client's material or hear it spoken. It's useful to keep the client's goals in mind, and to speak to them, because this helps reduce defensiveness. "I have a question that I hope will help me better understand how you can be less distracted by thoughts about work when you are with your children," a coach might say, knowing this is one of his client's goals. Whatever question the coach asks next, it's bound to be received with greater openness than had the coach simply jumped right in without linking it to what the client cares about. At the same time, respect privacy and preferences for how much your client is willing to bare.

Coaching can be either directive or nondirective. Directive coaching involves listening to your client and then offering advice from your own experiences or knowledge base. Nondirective coaching requires listening to your client's problems, but instead of then offering advice, asking questions that encourage your client to reach solutions independently. Asking good questions helps your client achieve greater self-understanding. Both forms of coaching can be effective; the preferred type depends on client needs. You'll likely find yourself switching between providing (and receiving) directive and nondirective coaching as your coaching partnership develops and as you learn more about the other members of your network.

Mind the Four C's

No matter which style of coaching you are engaging in at any point along the way, as both coach and client it's useful to keep in mind these four core values to make a coaching exchange work for everyone's benefit—be curious, collaborative, committed, and compassionate.

Be Curious

Being curious means trying to avoid making assumptions about what the other members in your coaching network really mean, want, or need and instead asking genuine questions that encourage your clients to explain what they're thinking and feeling. Open-ended questions are essential. For example, "Do you two enjoy spending time with each other's in-laws?" may yield a different (and too narrowly constrained) answer than, "How would each of you describe your relationship with your in-laws?" Asking questions that aim to probe at the root of a statement, rather than a proposed path forward, helps encourage your clients to discover options neither of you might have considered on your own. The general principle that seems to work well is this: ask for more detail, request examples, and pose questions such as "what if?" And then listen and follow up with more questions that demonstrate your interest. The more curious you can be, the more you'll learn about your coaching partner's true situation, and the more you'll be able to be helpful.

Be Collaborative

Coaching exchanges require an attitude of collaboration—we're all in this together. The goal in participating in this coaching network is to support one another in the fulfillment of your individual and shared dreams and to work in concert for the benefit of your children, your careers, and your lives together. People tend to fear change because it forces them into unknown territory, where life is unpredictable. Having the support of a coaching partnership and knowing your coaches are there to help you—in identifying the need for specific kinds of change, making the decision to act, designing new ways of trying things, reinforcing movement, and reflecting on what's working and what's not—adds value for everyone. Coaching exchanges work best when all parties enter the relationship knowing they have to be both giving and receiving help, in about equal measure. This makes it feel like a truly collaborative enterprise.

Be Committed

Before you join a coaching network, and then again during or just after your first meeting, consider whether or not you are able to provide what's expected and if the other members are in turn able to do the same. It's useful to talk briefly, for example, about what each member expects in terms of frequency of contact. Does one hope to meet weekly while another would be happier with monthly? Can you and your partner keep up with the reading and exercises schedule planned out by the group? The clearer you are about what level of commitment you can provide to your coaching partners, the smoother the process will be. Once you agree on rules of engagement for your coaching network—which, of course, you can always adjust as you learn more about what's working—then the real fun begins. The satisfaction you feel from seeing how your efforts are benefiting someone else is contagious. We find that commitment begets commitment in a coaching exchange. The more each coach demonstrates their willingness to provide support, encouragement, and sometimes a gentle nudge or swift kick, the more others are motivated to do the same. It's an upward spiral from which everyone benefits.

Be Compassionate

In coaching exchanges about the topics we ask you to address, there is the potential for conflict. Differences in approaches to parenting and to all kinds of life decisions may emerge. Your role as a coach to another parenting partnership is to be compassionate by listening, supporting, and encouraging your clients—doing your best to suspend judgment. Accept that you do not need to, and very likely will not, agree with everything your clients say or do. You can have different goals and values and still support other parents as they strive to live their lives together. Try to understand and respect your differences. Remember that you are in this learning journey together, and everyone takes a different road. There are many ways to arrive at the same destination, and the way that works best for you may not make sense for someone else. Being a compassionate coach can help a client feel comfortable thinking deeply about tough questions and can make the difference between a client who remains stuck for fear of judgment and one who takes the leap to try a new way, knowing that their coach is there to care, whether or not that new way works out.

If you embody the four core values—curiosity, collaboration, commitment, and compassion—you're bound to have a productive and enjoyable coaching experience.

Notes

Preface

1. D. Katz and R. L. Kahn, *The Social Psychology of Organizations*, 2nd ed. (New York: Wiley, 1978); R. M. Kanter, *Work and Family in the United States: A Critical Review and Agenda for Research and Policy* (New York: Russell Sage Foundation, 1977); and L. Bailyn, "Career and Family Orientations of Husbands and Wives in Relation to Marital Happiness," *Human Relations* 23, no. 2 (1970): 97–113.

2. S. D. Friedman, "7 Policy Changes America Needs So People Can Work and Have Kids," *Harvard Business Review*, November 11, 2013, https://hbr.org/2013/11/7-policy-changes-america-needs-so-people-can-work-and-have-kids.

3. An enormous amount of literature is emerging on this last issue. See, for but one example, D. Wallace-Wells, *The Uninhabitable Earth: Life after Warming* (New York: Tim Duggan Books, 2019); and visit https://www.un.org/en/climate change/reports.shtml for the United Nations Climate Reports.

Chapter 1

1. S. D. Friedman, P. Christensen, and J. DeGroot, "Work and Life: The End of the Zero-Sum Game," *Harvard Business Review*, November–December 1998, 119–130.

2. M. Hammond, R. Clapp-Smith, and M. Palanski, "Beyond (Just) the Work-place: A Theory of Leader Development across Multiple Domains," *Academy of Management Review* 42, no. 3 (2017): 481–498.

3. We'll be focusing a lot of attention on building trust throughout this book, for it is the very currency of leadership. The more trust surrounding us as leaders, the more readily we can move with support toward our vision. For a comprehensive overview of research on this concept, see K. T. Dirks and D. L. Ferrin, "Trust in Leadership: Meta-analytic Findings and Implications for Research and Practice," *Journal of Applied Psychology* 87, no. 4 (2002): 611–628.

4. This is a core concept in clinical psychology, described in various classic works, including, for example, C. R. Rogers, *On Becoming a Person: A Therapist's View of Psychotherapy* (New York: Houghton Mifflin Harcourt, 1961).

5. Ellen Galinsky's landmark study on how children see their parents' working lives inspired our use of this phrase as a chapter title. E. Galinsky, *Ask the Children: What America's Children Really Think about Working Parents* (New York: William Morrow, 1999).

6. For recent discussions of finding purpose through work, see A. M. Carton, "'I'm Not Mopping the Floors, I'm Putting a Man on the Moon': How NASA Leaders

Enhanced the Meaningfulness of Work by Changing the Meaning of Work," *Administrative Science Quarterly* 63, no. 2 (2018): 323–369; Harvard Business Review, *Purpose, Meaning, and Passion* (Boston: Harvard Business Review Press, 2018); E. I. Lysova et al., "Fostering Meaningful Work in Organizations: A Multi-level Review and Integration," *Journal of Vocational Behavior* 110 (2019): 374–389.

7. For some evidence, see S. D. Friedman, "How Our Careers Affect Our Children," *Harvard Business Review*, November 14, 2018, https://hbr.org/2018/11/how-our-careers-affect-our-children; A. Grant, "Can Your Job Make You a More Controlling Parent?" *Salon*, July 15, 2018.

8. S. D. Friedman and J. J. Greenhaus, *Work and Families—Allies or Enemies? What Happens When Business Professionals Confront Life Choices* (Oxford, UK: Oxford University Press, 2000).

Chapter 2

1. J. Quoidbach, A. M. Wood, and M. Hansenne, "Back to the Future: The Effect of Daily Practice of Mental Time Travel into the Future on Happiness and Anxiety," *Journal of Positive Psychology* 4, no. 5 (2009): 349–355.

2. W. S. Crawford, M. J. Thompson, and B. E. Ashforth, "Work-Life Events Theory: Making Sense of Shock Events in Dual-Earner Couples," *Academy of Management Review* 44, no. 1 (2019): 194–212.

3. L. Parks-Leduc, G. Feldman, and A. Bardi, "Personality Traits and Personal Values: A Meta-analysis," *Personality and Social Psychology Review* 19, no. 1 (2015): 3–29.

4. T. A. Judge and R. F. Piccolo, "Transformational and Transactional Leadership: A Meta-analytic Test of Their Relative Validity," *Journal of Applied Psychology* 89, no. 5 (2004): 755–768.

5. J. E. Hoch et al., "Do Ethical, Authentic, and Servant Leadership Explain Variance Above and Beyond Transformational Leadership? A Meta-analysis," *Journal of Management* 44, no. 2 (2018): 501–529.

6. Hoch et al., "Do Ethical, Authentic, and Servant Leadership Explain Variance Above and Beyond Transformational Leadership?"; G. Wang et al., "Transformational Leadership and Performance across Criteria and Levels: A Meta-analytic Review of 25 Years of Research," *Group & Organization Management* 36, no. 2 (2011): 223–270; M. Weiss et al., "Authentic Leadership and Leaders' Mental Well-being: An Experience Sampling Study," *The Leadership Quarterly* 29, no. 2 (2018): 309–321.

7. G. Albanese, G. De Blasio, and P. Sestito, "My Parents Taught Me. Evidence on the Family Transmission of Values," *Journal of Population Economics* 29, no. 2 (2016): 571–592.

8. A. Galinsky and M. Schweitzer, *Friend & Foe: When to Cooperate, When to Compete, and How to Succeed at Both* (New York: Crown Business, 2015).

9. B. Verplanken and R. W. Holland, "Motivated Decision Making: Effects of Activation and Self-Centrality of Values on Choices and Behavior," *Journal of Personality and Social Psychology* 82, no. 3 (2002): 434–447.

10. D. A. Kenny and L. K. Acitelli, "Accuracy and Bias in the Perception of the Partner in a Close Relationship," *Journal of Personality and Social Psychology* 80, no. 3 (2001): 439–448.

11. S. D. Friedman, *Total Leadership: Be a Better Leader, Have a Richer Life* (Boston: Harvard Business Review Press, 2008).

12. S. J. Ashford and D. S. DeRue, "Developing as a Leader: The Power of Mindful Engagement," *Organizational Dynamics* 41, no. 2 (2012): 146–154.

13. R. E. Boyatzis and K. Akrivou, "The Ideal Self as the Driver of Intentional Change," *Journal of Management Development* 25, no. 7 (2006): 624–642; R. E. Boyatzis, K. Rochford, and S. N. Taylor, "The Role of the Positive Emotional Attractor in Vision and Shared Vision: Toward Effective Leadership, Relationships, and Engagement," *Frontiers in Psychology* 6 (2015): 670.

14. Quoidbach et al., "Back to the Future"; see also S. D. Friedman, *Leading the Life You Want: Skills for Integrating Work and Life* (Boston: Harvard Business Review Press, 2014); M. E. Seligman, *Authentic Happiness: Using the New Positive Psychology to Realize Your Potential for Lasting Fulfillment* (New York: Simon and Schuster, 2004); M. L. Kringelbach and K. C. Berridge, "The Neuroscience of Happiness and Pleasure," *Social Research* 77, no. 2 (2010): 659–678.

15. A. M. Carton, C. Murphy, and J. R. Clark, "A (Blurry) Vision of the Future: How Leader Rhetoric about Ultimate Goals Influences Performance," *Academy of Management Journal* 57, no. 6 (2014): 1544–1570.

16. Y. Berson et al., "Leading from Different Psychological Distances: A Construal-level Perspective on Vision Communication, Goal Setting, and Follower Motivation," *The Leadership Quarterly* 26, no. 2 (2015): 143–155.

17. M. Valcour, "The Dual-Career Mojo That Makes Couples Thrive," *Harvard Business Review*, April 11, 2013, https://hbr.org/2013/04/the-dual-career-mojo-that-make.

18. W. Wood and D. Rünger, "Psychology of Habit," *Annual Review of Psychology* 67 (2016): 289–314.

19. J. S. Hammond, R. L. Keeney, and H. Raiffa, "The Hidden Traps in Decision Making," *Harvard Business Review*, September–October 1998, 47–58.

20. Carton et al., "A (Blurry) Vision of the Future."

21. A. M. Passarelli, "Vision-Based Coaching: Optimizing Resources for Leader Development," *Frontiers in Psychology* 6 (2015): 412.

22. Carton et al., "A (Blurry) Vision of the Future."

23. W. S. Crawford et al., "Work-Life Events Theory: Making Sense of Shock Events in Dual-Earner Couples."

24. Carton et al., "A (Blurry) Vision of the Future."

Chapter 3

1. S. D. Friedman, P. Christensen, and J. DeGroot, "Work and Life: The End of the Zero-Sum Game," *Harvard Business Review*, November–December 1998, 119–130.

2. L. M. Leslie, E. B. King, and J. A. Clair, "Work-Life Ideologies: The Contextual Basis and Consequences of Beliefs about Work and Life," *Academy of Management Review* 44, no. 1 (2019): 72–98.

3. S. J. Ashford and D. S. DeRue, "Developing as a Leader: The Power of Mindful Engagement," *Organizational Dynamics* 41, no. 2 (2012): 146–154; S. D. Friedman, *Leading the Life You Want: Skills for Integrating Work and Life* (Boston: Harvard Business Review Press, 2014).

4. M. Gubler, J. Arnold, and C. Coombs, "Reassessing the Protean Career Concept: Empirical Findings, Conceptual Components, and Measurement," *Journal of Organizational Behavior* 35, no. S1 (2014): S23–S40; M. Gubler, J. Arnold, and C. Coombs, "Organizational Boundaries and Beyond: A New Look at the Components of a Boundaryless Career Orientation," *Career Development International* 19, no. 6 (2014): 641–667; P. M. Bal, M. Van Kleef, and P. G. W. Jansen, "The Impact of Career Customization on Work Outcomes: Boundary Conditions of Manager Support and Employee Age," *Journal of Organizational Behavior* 36, no. 3 (2015): 421–440.

5. C. Bailey and A. Madden, "What Makes Work Meaningful—or Meaningless?" *MIT Sloan Management Review* 57, no. 4 (2016): 53–61; R. D. Duffy and B. J. Dik, "Research on Calling: What Have We Learned and Where Are We Going?" *Journal of Vocational Behavior* 83, no. 3 (2013): 428–436.

6. Bureau of Labor Statistics, "Table 8B. Time Spent in Primary Activities for the Civilian Population 18 Years and Over by Presence and Age of Youngest Household Child and Sex, 2017 Annual Averages, Employed," June 28, 2018, www.bls.gov.

7. L. Gratton and A. Scott, *The 100-Year Life: Living and Working in an Age of Longevity* (London: Bloomsbury Information, 2016).

8. F. S. Luyster et al., "Sleep: A Health Imperative," *Sleep* 35, no. 6 (2012): 727–734.

9. There is a large amount of literature on this issue. See, for example, B. M. Altevogt and H. R. Colten, eds., *Sleep Disorders and Sleep Deprivation: An Unmet Public Health Problem* (Washington, DC: National Academies Press, 2006). Arianna Huffington has done much to popularize the importance of sleep, including: A. Huffington, *The Sleep Revolution: Transforming Your Life, One Night at a Time* (New York: Harmony, 2016); J. C. Williams et al., *Stable Scheduling Study: Health Outcomes Report* (San Francisco: University of California Hastings College of the Law, 2019).

10. L. Vanderkam, *Off the Clock: Feel Less Busy While Getting More Done* (New York: Portfolio/Penguin, 2018).

11. A. A. Bennett, A. B. Bakker, and J. G. Field, "Recovery from Work-Related Effort: A Meta-analysis," *Journal of Organizational Behavior* 39, no. 3 (2018): 262–275.

12. S. Sonnentag, L. Venz, and A. Casper, "Advances in Recovery Research: What Have We Learned? What Should Be Done Next?" *Journal of Occupational Health Psychology* 22, no. 3 (2017): 365–380.

13. S. Gottfried, "Niksen Is the Dutch Lifestyle Concept of Doing Nothing—and You're About to See It Everywhere," *Time*, July 12, 2019, https://time.com/5622094/what-is-niksen/.

14. S. Sonnentag, "Work, Recovery Activities, and Individual Well-being: A Diary Study," *Journal of Occupational Health Psychology* 6, no. 3 (2001): 196–210.

15. For a few examples of research on this topic, see T. W. Ng and D. C. Feldman, "Long Work Hours: A Social Identity Perspective on Meta-analysis Data," *Journal of Organizational Behavior* 29 no. 7 (2008): 853–880; M. Kivimäki et al., "Long Working Hours and Risk of Coronary Heart Disease and Stroke: A Systematic Review and Meta-analysis of Published and Unpublished Data for 603,838 Individuals," *Lancet* 386, no. 10005 (2015): 1739–1746; C. Nohe et al., "The Chicken or the Egg? A Meta-analysis of Panel Studies of the Relationship between Work–Family Conflict and Strain," *Journal of Applied Psychology* 100, no. 2 (2015): 522–536; I. Martinez-Corts et al., "Spillover of Interpersonal Conflicts from Work into Nonwork: A Daily Diary Study," *Journal of Occupational Health Psychology* 20, no. 3 (2015): 326–337; D. Unger et al., "The Longer Your Work Hours, the Worse Your Relationship? The Role of Selective Optimization with Compensation in the Associations of Working Time with Relationship Satisfaction and Self-Disclosure in Dual-Career Couples," *Human Relations* 68, no. 12 (2015): 1889–1912.

16. D. Du, D. Derks, and A. B. Bakker, "Daily Spillover from Family to Work: A Test of the Work–Home Resources Model," *Journal of Occupational Health Psychology* 23, no. 2 (2018): 237–247; J. J. Hakanen and A. B. Bakker, "Born and Bred to Burn Out: A Life-Course View and Reflections on Job Burnout," *Journal of Occupational Health Psychology* 22, no. 3 (2017): 354–364; P. S. Wang et al., "Effects of Major Depression on Moment-in-Time Work Performance," *American Journal of Psychiatry* 161, no. 10 (2004): 1885–1891; M. T. Ford et al., "Relationships between Psychological, Physical, and Behavioural Health and Work Performance: A Review and Meta-analysis," *Work & Stress* 25, no. 3 (2011): 185–204; L. Loutzenhiser, P. McAuslan, and D. P. Sharpe, "The Trajectory of Maternal and Paternal Fatigue and Factors Associated with Fatigue across the Transition to Parenthood," *Clinical Psychologist* 19, no. 1 (2015): 15–27.

17. N. P. Rothbard, "Enriching or Depleting? The Dynamics of Engagement in Work and Family Roles," *Administrative Science Quarterly* 46, no. 4 (2001): 655–684. See also S. D. Friedman and J. H. Greenhaus, *Work and Family—Allies or Enemies? What Happens When Business Professionals Confront Life Choices* (New York: Oxford University Press, 2000); J. H. Greenhaus and G. N. Powell, "When Work and Family Are Allies: A Theory of Work-Family Enrichment," *Academy of Management Review* 31, no. 1 (2006): 72–92.

18. J. I. Menges et al., "When Job Performance Is All Relative: How Family Motivation Energizes Effort and Compensates for Intrinsic Motivation," *Academy of Management Journal* 60, no. 2 (2017): 695–719.

19. Y. Zhang et al., "The Within and Cross Domain Effects of Work-Family Enrichment: A Meta-analysis," *Journal of Vocational Behavior* 104 (2018): 210–227.

20. A. H. Huffman, W. J. Casper, and S. C. Payne, "How Does Spouse Career Support Relate to Employee Turnover? Work Interfering with Family and Job Satisfaction as Mediators," *Journal of Organizational Behavior* 35, no. 2 (2014): 194–212; M. Ferguson et al., "The Supportive Spouse at Work: Does Being Work-Linked Help?" *Journal of Occupational Health Psychology* 21, no. 1 (2016): 37–50.

21. Y. Tang, X. Huang, and Y. Wang, "Good Marriage at Home, Creativity at Work: Family–Work Enrichment Effect on Workplace Creativity," *Journal of Organizational Behavior* 38, no. 5 (2017): 749–766.

22. B. C. Feeney and N. L. Collins, "A New Look at Social Support: A Theoretical Perspective on Thriving through Relationships," *Personality and Social Psychology Review* 19, no. 2 (2015): 113–147; P. R. Pietromonaco and N. L. Collins, "Interpersonal Mechanisms Linking Close Relationships to Health," *American Psychologist* 72, no. 6 (2017): 531–542.

23. S. M. Southwick and D. S. Charney, "The Science of Resilience: Implications for the Prevention and Treatment of Depression," *Science* 338, no. 6103 (2012): 79–82.

24. J. Stoeber and K. Otto, "Positive Conceptions of Perfectionism: Approaches, Evidence, Challenges," *Personality and Social Psychology Review* 10, no. 4 (2006): 295–319. For a more in-depth approach to understanding and managing perfectionism, see B. Brown, *The Gifts of Imperfection: Let Go of Who You Think You're Supposed to Be and Embrace Who You Are* (Center City, MN: Hazelden Publishing, 2010).

25. D. Kahneman, J. L. Knetsch, and R. H. Thaler, "Anomalies: The Endowment Effect, Loss Aversion, and Status Quo Bias," *Journal of Economic Perspectives* 5, no. 1 (1991): 193–206.

26. S. Eidelman and C. S. Crandall, "Bias in Favor of the Status Quo," *Social and Personality Psychology Compass* 6, no. 3 (2012): 270–281. For a deeper dive into cognitive biases, consider reading D. Kahneman, *Thinking, Fast and Slow* (New York: Farrar, Straus and Giroux, 2011); D. Ariely, *Predictably Irrational: The Hidden Forces That Shape Our Decisions* (New York: HarperCollins, 2008); B. Schwartz, *The Paradox of Choice: Why More Is Less* (New York: Harper Perennial, 2005).

27. D. D. Burns, *Feeling Good: The New Mood Therapy* (New York: William Morrow, 1999).

28. M. Russo et al., "Boundary Management Permeability and Relationship Satisfaction in Dual-Earner Couples: The Asymmetrical Gender Effect," *Frontiers in Psychology* 9 (2018): 1723; K. S. Wilson et al., "Misery Loves Company: An Investigation of Couples' Interrole Conflict Congruence," *Academy of Management Journal* 61, no. 2 (2018): 715–737.

29. Z. Song, M. D. Foo, and M. A. Uy, "Mood Spillover and Crossover Among Dual-Earner Couples: A Cell Phone Event Sampling Study," *Journal of Applied Psychology* 93, no. 2 (2008): 443–452; Z. Song et al., "Unraveling the Daily Stress Crossover between Unemployed Individuals and Their Employed Spouses," *Journal of Applied Psychology* 96, no. 1 (2011): 151–168; M. Ferguson, "You Cannot Leave It at the Office: Spillover and Crossover of Coworker Incivility," *Journal of Organizational Behavior* 33, no. 4 (2012): 571–588; D. S. Carlson, M. J. Thompson, and K. M. Kacmar, "Double Crossed: The Spillover and Crossover Effects of Work Demands on Work Outcomes through the Family," *Journal of Applied Psychology* 104, no. 2 (2018): 214–228; D. S. Carlson et al., "Spillover and Crossover of Work Resources: A Test of the Positive Flow of Resources through Work–Family Enrichment," *Journal of Organizational Behavior* 40, no. 6 (2019): 709–722.

30. A. B. Bakker, E. Demerouti, and M. F. Dollard, "How Job Demands Affect Partners' Experience of Exhaustion: Integrating Work-Family Conflict and Crossover Theory," *Journal of Applied Psychology* 93, no. 4 (2008): 901–911; L. L. ten Brummelhuis and J. H. Greenhaus, "How Role Jugglers Maintain Relationships at Home and at Work: A Gender Comparison," *Journal of Applied Psychology* 103, no. 12 (2018): 1265–1282.

31. A. Rodríguez-Muñoz et al., "Engaged at Work and Happy at Home: A Spillover–Crossover Model," *Journal of Happiness Studies* 15, no. 2 (2014): 271–283.

32. Ten Brummelhuis and Greenhaus, "How Role Jugglers Maintain Relationships at Home and at Work."

33. S. D. Friedman, *Total Leadership: Be a Better Leader, Have a Richer Life* (Boston: Harvard Business Review Press, 2008).

34. J. Zaki, "Empathy: A Motivated Account," *Psychological Bulletin* 140, no. 6 (2014): 1608–1647.

35. For a discussion of the importance of spending time outside the romantic relationship to make it more interesting and exciting, see S. Pileggi Pawelski and J. O. Pawelski, *Happy Together: Using the Science of Positive Psychology to Build Love That Lasts* (New York: TarcherPerigee, 2018).

36. Sources for these ideas include S. Scott, *Fierce Conversations: Achieving Success at Work and in Life, One Conversation at a Time* (New York: Berkley, 2004); R. Schwarz, *Smart Leaders, Smarter Teams: How You and Your Team Get Unstuck to Get Results* (San Francisco: Jossey-Bass, 2013).

Chapter 4

1. A. Waldman, *Bad Mother: A Chronicle of Maternal Crimes, Minor Calamities, and Occasional Moments of Grace* (New York: Doubleday, 2009).

2. For a richly informative study that directly addresses this, see E. Galinsky, *Ask the Children: What America's Children Really Think About Working Parents* (New York: William Morrow, 1999).

3. More on the social, economic, and political contexts of parenting can be found in the following books. About motherhood: J. C. Williams and R. Dempsey, *What Works for Women at Work: Four Patterns Working Women Need to Know* (New York: New York University Press, 2014); C. Collins, *Making Motherhood Work: How Women Manage Careers and Caregiving* (Princeton, NJ: Princeton University Press, 2019); A. Westervelt, *Forget "Having It All": How America Messed Up Motherhood—and How to Fix It* (New York: Seal Press, 2018); S. Sandberg, *Lean In: Women, Work, and the Will to Lead* (New York: Alfred A. Knopf, 2013). About fatherhood: J. Levs, *All In: How Our Work-First Culture Fails Dads, Families, and Businesses—and How We Can Fix It Together* (New York: HarperCollins, 2015); S. Behson, *The Working Dad's Survival Guide: How to Succeed at Work and at Home* (Melbourne, FL: Motivational Press, 2015); *The New Dad* series of studies (http://thenewdad.org) from the Center for Work and Family at the Carroll School of Management, Boston College.

4. J. J. Ladge and D. Greenberg, *Maternal Optimism: Forging Positive Paths through Work and Motherhood* (New York: Oxford University Press, 2019).

5. S. D. Friedman and J. H. Greenhaus, *Work and Family—Allies or Enemies? What Happens When Business Professionals Confront Life Choices* (New York: Oxford University Press, 2000).

6. E. Reid, "Embracing, Passing, Revealing, and the Ideal Worker Image: How People Navigate Expected and Experienced Professional Identities," *Organization Science* 26, no. 4 (2015): 997–1017.

7. T. L. Dumas and J. Sanchez-Burks, "The Professional, the Personal, and the Ideal Worker: Pressures and Objectives Shaping the Boundary between Life Domains," *Academy of Management Annals* 9, no. 1 (2015): 803–843; K. Christopher, "Extensive Mothering: Employed Mothers' Constructions of the Good Mother," *Gender & Society* 26, no. 1 (2012): 73–96; K. Bahler, "Girls with Working Moms Get Better Jobs and Higher Pay, According to Research," *Time*, May 10, 2018.

8. T. W. Ng and D. C. Feldman, "Long Work Hours: A Social Identity Perspective on Meta-analysis Data," *Journal of Organizational Behavior* 29, no. 7 (2008): 853–880.

9. Friedman and Greenhaus, *Work and Family—Allies or Enemies?*; Ladge and Greenberg, *Maternal Optimism*.

10. A. Wrzesniewski et al., "Jobs, Careers, and Callings: People's Relations to Their Work," *Journal of Research in Personality* 31, no. 1 (1997): 21–33.

11. D. S. Carlson et al., "Measuring the Positive Side of the Work–Family Interface: Development and Validation of a Work–Family Enrichment Scale," *Journal of Vocational Behavior* 68, no. 1 (2006): 131–164.

12. R. Ilies et al., "When Can Employees Have a Family Life? The Effects of Daily Workload and Affect on Work-Family Conflict and Social Behaviors at Home," *Journal of Applied Psychology* 92, no. 5 (2007): 1368–1379; R. Ilies et al., "Why Do Employees Have Better Family Lives When They Are Highly Engaged at Work?" *Journal of Applied Psychology* 102, no. 6 (2017): 956–970.

13. D. P. Bhave and A. M. Lefter, "The Other Side: Occupational Interactional Requirements and Work–Home Enrichment," *Academy of Management Journal* 61, no. 1 (2018): 139–164.

14. For compelling approaches for understanding and managing this issue, see C. Newport, *Digital Minimalism: Choosing a Focused Life in a Noisy World* (New York: Portfolio/Penguin, 2019); S. Turkle, *Reclaiming Conversation: The Power of Talk in a Digital Age* (New York: Penguin Press, 2015); A. Alter, *Irresistible: The Rise of Addictive Technology and the Business of Keeping Us Hooked* (New York: Penguin Press, 2017).

15. B. T. McDaniel and J. S. Radesky, "Technoference: Parent Distraction with Technology and Associations with Child Behavior Problems," *Child Development* 89, no. 1 (2018): 100–109; B. McDaniel et al., " 'Technoference' and Implications for Mothers' and Fathers' Couple and Coparenting Relationship Quality," *Computers in Human Behavior* 80 (2018): 303–313; C. Steiner-Adair, *The Big Disconnect: Protecting Childhood and Family Relationships in the Digital Age* (New York: Harper, 2013).

16. J. M. Twenge, W. K. Campbell, and C. A. Foster, "Parenthood and Marital Satisfaction: A Meta-analytic Review," *Journal of Marriage and Family* 65, no. 3 (2003): 574–583.

17. B. D. Doss et al., "The Effect of the Transition to Parenthood on Relationship Quality: An 8-Year Prospective Study," *Journal of Personality and Social Psychology* 96, no. 3 (2009): 601–619.

18. S. K. Nelson, K. Kushlev, and S. Lyubomirsky, "The Pains and Pleasures of Parenting: When, Why, and How Is Parenthood Associated with More or Less Well-Being?" *Psychological Bulletin* 140, no. 3 (2014): 846–895.

19. S. Friedman, *Neil Blumenthal: Sacred Time*, Episode 83, July 25, 2018, www.workandlifepodcast.com.

20. Pew Research Center, "Raising Kids and Running a Household: How Working Parents Share the Load," November 4, 2015, www.pewsocialtrends.org.

21. Among the enumerable resources available on dual-career relationships, noteworthy are: J. Petriglieri, *Couples That Work: How Dual-Career Couples Can Thrive in Love and Work* (Boston: Harvard Business Review Press, 2019); and R. C. Barnett and C. Rivers, *She Works/He Works: How Two-Income Families Are Happier, Healthier, and Better Off* (New York: HarperCollins, 1996).

22. B. D. Doss and G. K. Rhoades, "The Transition to Parenthood: Impact on Couples' Romantic Relationships," *Current Opinion in Psychology* 13 (2017): 25–28.

23. Y. Luo et al., "Grandparents Providing Care to Grandchildren: A Population-Based Study of Continuity and Change," *Journal of Family Issues* 33, no. 9 (2012): 1143–1167.

24. J. Lim and D. F. Dinges, "A Meta-analysis of the Impact of Short-Term Sleep Deprivation on Cognitive Variables," *Psychological Bulletin* 136, no. 3 (2010): 375–389.

25. P. Philip and T. Åkerstedt, "Transport and Industrial Safety, How Are They Affected by Sleepiness and Sleep Restriction?" *Sleep Medicine Reviews* 10, no. 5 (2006): 347–356.

26. C. A. Yao and R. E. Rhodes, "Parental Correlates in Child and Adolescent Physical Activity: A Meta-analysis," *International Journal of Behavioral Nutrition and Physical Activity* 12, no. 10 (2015): 1–38.

27. E. Faught et al. "The Influence of Parental Encouragement and Caring About Healthy Eating on Children's Diet Quality and Body Weights," *Public Health Nutrition* 19, no. 5 (2016): 822–829.

28. Friedman and Greenhaus, *Work and Family—Allies or Enemies?*

29. J. Parent et al., "Parent Mindfulness and Child Outcome: The Roles of Parent Depressive Symptoms and Parenting," *Mindfulness* 1, no. 4 (2010): 254–264.

30. J. D. Coatsworth et al., "Integrating Mindfulness with Parent Training: Effects of the Mindfulness-Enhanced Strengthening Families Program," *Developmental Psychology* 51, no. 1 (2015): 26–35.; Friedman and Greenhaus, *Work and Family—Allies or Enemies?*

31. Though this was probably more about who you wanted to be than what you wanted to do, according to this informative review of decision-making as it relates to choosing to become a parent. J. Rothman, "The Art of Decision-Making," *New Yorker*, January 21, 2019.

32. There is an enormous amount of literature on parenting and child development, and we cannot review it all here. Our ideas draw primarily on these sources:

T. B. Brazelton and S. I. Greenspan, *The Irreducible Needs of Children: What Every Child Must Have to Grow, Learn, and Flourish* (Boston: Lifelong Books, 2009): E. Galinsky, *Mind in the Making: The Seven Essential Life Skills Every Child Needs* (New York: HarperStudio, 2010); D. J. Siegel and T. P. Bryson, *The Whole-Brain Child: 12 Proven Strategies to Nurture Your Child's Developing Mind* (New York: Bantam Books, 2012).

33. A. M. Groh et al., "Attachment in the Early Life Course: Meta-analytic Evidence for Its Role in Socioemotional Development," *Child Development Perspectives* 11, no. 1 (2017): 70–76.

34. C. Kandler, J. Gottschling, and F. M. Spinath, "Genetic and Environmental Parent–Child Transmission of Value Orientations: An Extended Twin Family Study," *Child Development* 87, no. 1 (2016): 270–284.

35. N. Eisenberg, "Emotion, Regulation, and Moral Development," *Annual Review of Psychology* 51, no. 1 (2000): 665–697.

36. B. D. Bugental and C. Johnston, "Parental and Child Cognitions in the Context of the Family," *Annual Review of Psychology* 51, no. 1 (2000): 315–344; R. D. Parke, "Development in the Family," *Annual Review of Psychology* 55 (2004): 365–399.

37. B. Schulte, "Making Time for Kids? Study Says Quality Trumps Quality," *Washington Post*, March 28, 2015.

38. M. A. Milkie, K. M. Nomaguchi, and K. E. Denny, "Does the Amount of Time Mothers Spend with Children or Adolescents Matter?" *Journal of Marriage and Family* 77, no. 2 (2015): 355–372; T. Cano, F. Perales, and J. Baxter, "A Matter of Time: Father Involvement and Child Cognitive Outcomes," *Journal of Marriage and Family* 81 (2019): 164–184. The research on quality versus quantity, however, is not entirely clear. See, for instance, P. Fomby and K. Musick, "Mothers' Time, the Parenting Package, and Links to Healthy Child Development," *Journal of Marriage and Family* 80, no. 1 (2018): 166–181.

39. Z. Liu et al., "Leader Development Begins at Home: Overparenting Harms Adolescent Leader Emergence," *Journal of Applied Psychology* 104, no. 10 (2019): 1226–1242. For a recent journalistic account on the importance of play, see K. Brooks, "We Have Ruined Childhood," *New York Times*, August 17, 2019.

40. For important treatments of this topic, see S. H. Fraiberg, *The Magic Years: Understanding and Handling the Problems of Early Childhood* (New York: Scribner's, 1959); and E. Tronick, *The Neurobehavioral and Social-Emotional Development of Infants and Children* (New York: W. W. Norton & Company, 2007).

41. A. Biglan et al., "The Critical Role of Nurturing Environments for Promoting Human Well-Being," *American Psychologist* 67, no. 4 (2012): 257–271.

42. E. T. Gershoff, "Corporal Punishment by Parents and Associated Child Behaviors and Experiences: A Meta-analytic and Theoretical Review," *Psychological Bulletin* 128, no. 4 (2002): 539–579.

43. R. D. Parke, "Development in the Family," *Annual Review of Psychology* 55, no. 1 (2004): 365–399.

44. The nine steps for speaking "Freddish" were enumerated in M. King, "Mr. Rogers Had a Simple Set of Rules for Talking to Children," *The Atlantic*, June 8, 2018.

45. For example, A. Grant and A. S. Grant, *The Gift Inside the Box* (New York: Dial Books, 2019); C. McCloud, *Have You Filled a Bucket Today? A Guide to Daily Happiness for Kids* (West Bloomfield, MI: Bucket Philosophies, 2015); M. Agassi, *Hands Are Not for Hitting* (Golden Valley, MN: Free Spirit Publishing, 2002).

46. Renowned child psychologist Laurel Silber, personal communication.

Chapter 5

1. There is an enormous and rapidly growing amount of literature about how relationships at work and in our families affect each other and what can be done to make these connections mutually beneficial. Some of this research is cited in this chapter. Interested readers should consult these books: A. M. Slaughter, *Unfinished Business: Women, Men, Work, Family* (New York: Random House, 2015); B. Schulte, *Overwhelmed: How to Work, Love, and Play When No One Has the Time* (New York: Sarah Crichton Books, 2014); J. Pfeffer, *Dying for a Paycheck: How Modern Management Harms Employee Health and Company Performance—and What We Can Do About It* (New York: Harper Business, 2018); L. A. Perlow, *Sleeping with Your Smart Phone: How to Break the 24/7 Habit and Change the Way You Work* (Boston: Harvard Business Review Press, 2012).

2. D. M Almeida et al., "Supervisor Support Buffers Daily Psychological and Physiological Reactivity to Work-to-Family Conflict," *Journal of Marriage and Family* 78, no. 1 (2016): 165–179.

3. R. A. Matthews et al., "Family-Supportive Supervisor Behaviors, Work Engagement, and Subjective Well-Being: A Contextually Dependent Mediated Process," *Journal of Occupational Health Psychology* 19, no. 2 (2014): 168–181; M. Russo et al., "When Family Supportive Supervisors Meet Employees' Need for Caring: Implications for Work–Family Enrichment and Thriving," *Journal of Management* 44, no. 4 (2018): 1678–1702.

4. E. E. Kossek and A. Friede, "The Business Case: Managerial Perspectives on Work and the Family," in *The Work and Family Handbook: Multi-Disciplinary Perspectives, Methods, and Approaches* (Mahwah, NJ: Routledge, 2005), 611–626.

5. S. C. Eaton, "If You Can Use Them: Flexibility Policies, Organizational Commitment, and Perceived Performance," *Industrial Relations: A Journal of Economy and Society* 42, no. 2 (2003): 145–167; J. C. Williams, M. Blair-Loy, and J. L. Berdahl, "Cultural Schemas, Social Class, and the Flexibility Stigma," *Journal of Social Issues* 69, no. 2 (2013): 209–234; T. K. McNamara et al., "Access to and Utilization of Flexible Work Options," *Industrial Relations: A Journal of Economy and Society* 51, no. 4 (2012): 936–965.

6. L. B. Hammer et al. "Clarifying Work–Family Intervention Processes: The Roles of Work–Family Conflict and Family-Supportive Supervisor Behaviors," *Journal of Applied Psychology* 96, no. 1 (2011): 134–150.

7. L. B. Hammer et al., "Development and Validation of a Multidimensional Measure of Family Supportive Supervisor Behaviors (FSSB)," *Journal of Management* 35, no. 4 (2009): 837–856.

8. C. Liao, S. J. Wayne, and D. M. Rousseau, "Idiosyncratic Deals in Contemporary Organizations: A Qualitative and Meta-analytical Review," *Journal of Organizational Behavior* 37 (2016): S9–S29. And for another perspective on i-deals, see G. Lemmon et al., "A Cross-Domain Exploration of Performance Benefits and Costs of Idiosyncratic Deals," *Journal of Leadership & Organizational Studies* 23, no. 4 (2016): 440–455.

9. Hammer, "Development and Validation of a Multidimensional Measure of Family Supportive Supervisor Behaviors (FSSB)."

10. M. Bolino, D. Long, and W. Turnley, "Impression Management in Organizations: Critical Questions, Answers, and Areas for Future Research," *Annual Review of Organizational Psychology and Organizational Behavior* 3 (2016): 377–406.

11. U. R. Hülsheger and A. F. Schewe, "On the Costs and Benefits of Emotional Labor: A Meta-analysis of Three Decades of Research," *Journal of Occupational Health Psychology* 16, no. 3 (2011): 361–389; M. A. Krannitz et al., "Workplace Surface Acting and Marital Partner Discontent: Anxiety and Exhaustion Spillover Mechanisms," *Journal of Occupational Health Psychology* 20, no. 3 (2015): 314–325.

12. A. I. Emmerich and T. Rigotti, "Reciprocal Relations between Work-Related Authenticity and Intrinsic Motivation, Work Ability and Depressivity: A Two-Wave Study," *Frontiers in Psychology* 8 (2017): 307.

13. J. A. Kmec, "Are Motherhood Penalties and Fatherhood Bonuses Warranted? Comparing Pro-Work Behaviors and Conditions of Mothers, Fathers, and Non-Parents," *Social Science Research* 40, no. 2 (2011): 444–459.

14. A. Killewald, "A Reconsideration of the Fatherhood Premium: Marriage, Co-residence, Biology, and Fathers' Wages," *American Sociological Review* 78, no. 1 (2013): 96–116.

15. M. Gough and M. Noonan, "A Review of the Motherhood Wage Penalty in the United States," *Sociology Compass* 7, no. 4 (2013): 328–342.

16. J. Baldwin, "As Much Truth as One Can Bear," *New York Times*, January 14, 1962.

17. R. Martin et al., "Leader–Member Exchange (LMX) and Performance: A Meta-analytic Review," *Personnel Psychology* 69, no. 1 (2016): 67–121.

18. A. C. Edmondson and Z. Lei, "Psychological Safety: The History, Renaissance, and Future of an Interpersonal Construct," *Annual Review of Organizational Psychology and Organizational Behavior* 1, no. 1 (2014): 23–43.

19. D. Wademan Dowling, "How to Launch a Working Parents Support Group in Your Organization," *Harvard Business Review*, November 12, 2018, https://hbr.org/2018/11/how-to-launch-a-working-parents-support-group-in-your-organization.

20. R. I. Sutton, *The Asshole Survival Guide: How to Deal with People Who Treat You Like Dirt* (New York: Houghton Mifflin Harcourt, 2017).

21. H. G. Wolff and K. Moser, "Effects of Networking on Career Success: A Longitudinal Study," *Journal of Applied Psychology* 94, no. 1 (2009): 196–206.

22. Among the many useful books on this topic are W. E. Baker, *Achieving Success through Social Capital: Tapping the Hidden Resources in Your Per-*

sonal and Business Networks (San Francisco: Jossey-Bass, 2000); A. M. Grant, *Give and Take: Why Helping Others Drives Our Success* (New York: Viking, 2013); H. Ibarra, *Working Identity: Unconventional Strategies for Reinventing Your Career* (Boston: Harvard Business Review Press, 2003).

23. T. D. Allen et al., "Career Benefits Associated with Mentoring for Protégés: A Meta-analysis," *Journal of Applied Psychology* 89, no. 1 (2004): 127–136; R. Ghosh and T. G. Reid, Jr., "Career Benefits Associated with Mentoring for Mentors: A Meta-analysis," *Journal of Vocational Behavior* 83, no. 1 (2013): 106–116.

24. M. Jones, "Why Can't Companies Get Mentorship Programs Right?" *The Atlantic*, June 2, 2017.

25. A. Tjan, "What the Best Mentors Do," *Harvard Business Review*, February 27, 2017, https://hbr.org/2017/02/what-the-best-mentors-do.

26. D. Z. Levin, J. Walter, and J. K. Murnighan, "The Power of Reconnection—How Dormant Ties Can Surprise You," *MIT Sloan Management Review* 52, no. 3 (2011): 5–50.

27. For more on the work and nonwork benefits of job crafting, see: J. M. Berg, A. M. Grant, and V. Johnson, "When Callings Are Calling: Crafting Work and Leisure in Pursuit of Unanswered Occupational Callings," *Organization Science* 21, no. 5 (2010): 973–994; E. Demerouti, A. B. Bakker, and J. M. Gevers, "Job Crafting and Extra-Role Behavior: The Role of Work Engagement and Flourishing," *Journal of Vocational Behavior* 91 (2015): 87–96; M. Rastogi and R. Chaudhary, "Job Crafting and Work-Family Enrichment: The Role of Positive Intrinsic Work Engagement," *Personnel Review* 47, no. 3 (2018): 651–674; C. W. Rudolph et al., "Job Crafting: A Meta-analysis of Relationships with Individual Differences, Job Characteristics, and Work Outcomes," *Journal of Vocational Behavior* 102 (2017): 112–138.

Chapter 6

1. P. Parigi and W. Henson, "Social Isolation in America," *Annual Review of Sociology* 40 (2014): 153–171.

2. Pew Research Center, "Social Isolation and New Technology," November 4, 2009, www.pewsocialtrends.org.

3. P. A. Thoits, "Mechanisms Linking Social Ties and Support to Physical and Mental Health," *Journal of Health and Social Behavior* 52, no. 2 (2011): 145–161.

4. S. Cohen, "Social Relationships and Health," *American Psychologist* 59, no. 8 (2004): 676–684; B. J. Gillespie et al., "Close Adult Friendships, Gender, and the Life Cycle," *Journal of Social and Personal Relationships* 32, no. 6 (2015): 709–736.

5. R. Waldinger, "What Makes a Good Life? Lessons from the Longest Study on Happiness," TED talks, December 23, 2015, www.ted.com.

6. P. S. Adler and S. W. Kwon, "Social Capital: Prospects for a New Concept," *Academy of Management Review* 27, no. 1 (2002): 17–40.

7. K. L. Gilbert et al., "A Meta-Analysis of Social Capital and Health: A Case for Needed Research," *Journal of Health Psychology* 18, no. 11 (2013): 1385–1399; S. L. Dika and K. Singh, "Applications of Social Capital in Educational Literature:

A Critical Synthesis," *Review of Educational Research* 72, no. 1 (2002): 31–60; S. E. Seibert, M. L. Kraimer, and R. C. Liden, "A Social Capital Theory of Career Success," *Academy of Management Journal* 44, no. 2 (2001): 219–237.

8. C. L. Carmichael, H. T. Reis, and P. R. Duberstein, "In Your 20s It's Quantity, in Your 30s It's Quality: The Prognostic Value of Social Activity Across 30 Years of Adulthood," *Psychology and Aging* 30, no. 1 (2015): 95–105.

9. Pew Research Center, "The American Family Today," December 17, 2015, www.pewsocialtrends.org.

10. Bureau of Labor Statistics, "Table A-1. Time Spent in Detailed Primary Activities," 2017, www.bls.gov.

11. A. E. Colbert, J. E. Bono, and R. K. Purvanova, "Flourishing Via Workplace Relationships: Moving beyond Instrumental Support," *Academy of Management Journal* 59, no. 4 (2016): 1199–1223.

12. J. Pillemer and N. P. Rothbard, "Friends without Benefits: Understanding the Dark Sides of Workplace Friendship," *Academy of Management Review* 43, no. 4 (2018): 635–660.

13. J. C. Sullivan, "The Absolute Necessity of the New-Mom Friend, *New York Times*, August 18, 2018.

14. Bureau of Labor Statistics, "American Time Use Survey Summary," 2018, www.bls.gov.

15. P. Carneiro, K. V. Løken, and K. G. Salvanes, "A Flying Start? Maternity Leave Benefits and Long-Run Outcomes of Children," *Journal of Political Economy* 123, no. 2 (2015): 365–412; A. Hsin and C. Felfe, "When Does Time Matter? Maternal Employment, Children's Time with Parents, and Child Development," *Demography* 51, no. 5 (2014): 1867–1894. In a review of sixty-nine studies spanning five decades, Lucas-Thompson et al. found that mothers' employment did not affect children's academic achievement or behavioral problems. Moreover, in the instances where small differences did emerge, the outcomes favored the children of working mothers (e.g., when teacher ratings of achievement and behavior were used). R. G. Lucas-Thompson, W. A. Goldberg, and J. Prause, "Maternal Work Early in the Lives of Children and Its Distal Associations with Achievement and Behavior Problems: A Meta-analysis," *Psychological Bulletin* 136, no. 6 (2010): 915–942. Research comparing stay-at-home fathers with those who work outside the home is just beginning, so there is little accumulated evidence on the impact of stay-at-home dads. Pew Research Center, "Growing Number of Dads Home with the Kids," June 5, 2014, www.pewsocialtrends.org.

16. D. L. Vandell et al., "Do Effects of Early Child Care Extend to Age 15 Years? Results from the NICHD Study of Early Child Care and Youth Development," *Child Development* 81, no. 3 (2010): 737–756; N. Shpancer, "The Home–Daycare Link: Mapping Children's New World Order," *Early Childhood Research Quarterly* 17, no. 3 (2002): 374–392.

17. M. T. Wang and S. Sheikh-Khalil, "Does Parental Involvement Matter for Student Achievement and Mental Health in High School?" *Child Development* 85, no. 2 (2014): 610–625; W. Fan and C. M. Williams, "The Effects of Parental Involvement on Students' Academic Self-Efficacy, Engagement and Intrinsic Motivation," *Educational Psychology* 30, no. 1 (2010): 53–74.

18. H. H. Schiffrin et al., "Intensive Parenting: Does It Have the Desired Impact on Child Outcomes?" *Journal of Child and Family Studies* 24, no. 8 (2015): 2322–2331; C. Segrin et al., "The Association between Overparenting, Parent-Child Communication, and Entitlement and Adaptive Traits in Adult Children," *Family Relations* 61, no. 2 (2012): 237–252.

19. F. Martela and R. M. Ryan, "The Benefits of Benevolence: Basic Psychological Needs, Beneficence, and the Enhancement of Well-Being," *Journal of Personality* 84, no. 6 (2016): 750–764; J. A. Piliavin and E. Siegl, "Health Benefits of Volunteering in the Wisconsin Longitudinal Study," *Journal of Health and Social Behavior* 48, no. 4 (2007): 450–464.

20. P. C. Scales, P. L. Benson, and M. Mannes, "The Contribution to Adolescent Well-Being Made by Nonfamily Adults: An Examination of Developmental Assets as Contexts and Processes," *Journal of Community Psychology* 34, no. 4 (2006): 401–413.

21. L. Borden and J. Serido, "From Program Participant to Engaged Citizen: A Developmental Journey," *Journal of Community Psychology* 37, no. 4 (2009): 423–438.

22. T. K. Inagaki and E. Orehek, "On the Benefits of Giving Social Support: When, Why, and How Support Providers Gain by Caring for Others," *Current Directions in Psychological Science* 26, no. 2 (2017): 109–113.

23. Indeed, research has shown that the most intimate and supportive sibling relationships tend to be those with high degrees of conflict. K. Hank and A. Steinbach, "Intergenerational Solidarity and Intragenerational Relations between Adult Siblings," *Social Science Research* 76 (2018): 55–64.

24. M. Gilligan et al., "Family Networks and Psychological Well-Being in Midlife," *Social Sciences* 6, no. 3 (2017): 94.

25. G. D. Spitze and K. Trent, "Changes in Individual Sibling Relationships in Response to Life Events," *Journal of Family Issues* 39, no. 2 (2018): 503–526; L. White, "Sibling Relationships Over the Life Course: A Panel Analysis," *Journal of Marriage and Family* 63, no. 2 (2001): 555–568.

26. Pew Research Center, "The Sandwich Generation," January 30, 2013, www.pewsocialtrends.org; G. Spitze and K. Trent, "Gender Differences in Adult Sibling Relations in Two-Child Families," *Journal of Marriage and Family* 68, no. 4 (2006): 977–992; K. Pillemer and J. J. Suitor, "Who Provides Care? A Prospective Study of Caregiving Among Adult Siblings," *The Gerontologist* 54, no. 4 (2013): 589–598.

Chapter 7

1. Countless scholars have noted this, of course, including W. Bennis, *On Becoming a Leader* (Cambridge, MA: Perseus Publishing, 1989); R. A. Heifetz and M. Linsky, *Leadership on the Line: Staying Alive through the Dangers of Change* (Boston: Harvard Business Review Press, 2017); B. Brown, *Dare to Lead: Brave Work. Tough Conversations. Whole Hearts* (New York: Random House, 2018); N. M. Tichy and M. A. Devanna, *The Transformational Leader: The Key to Global Competitiveness* (New York: Wiley, 1997).

2. D. M. Herold et al., "The Effects of Transformational and Change Leadership on Employees' Commitment to a Change: A Multilevel Study," *Journal of Applied Psychology* 93, no. 2 (2008): 346–357. For a more in-depth discussion of change leadership, see B. Burnes, M. Hughes, and R. T. By, "Reimagining Organisational Change Leadership," *Leadership* 14, no. 2 (2018): 141–158; J. P. Kotter, *Leading Change* (Boston: Harvard Business Review Press, 2018); D. Ready, "4 Things Successful Change Leaders Do Well," *Harvard Business Review*, January 28, 2016, https://hbr.org/2016/01/4-things-successful-change-leaders-do-well.

3. Among the many books and articles on this topic are C. Duhigg, *The Power of Habit: Why We Do What We Do in Life and Business* (New York: Random House, 2012); and W. Wood and D. Rünger, "Psychology of Habit," *Annual Review of Psychology* 67 (2016): 289–314.

4. T. M. Amabile and S. J. Kramer, "The Power of Small Wins," *Harvard Business Review*, May 2011, 70–80; K. E. Weick, "Small Wins: Redefining the Scale of Social Problems," *American Psychologist* 39, no. 1 (1984): 40–49; S. B. Sitkin, "Learning through Failure: The Strategy of Small Losses," *Research in Organizational Behavior* 14 (1992): 231–266.

5. S. D. Friedman, *Total Leadership: Be a Better Leader, Have a Richer Life* (Boston: Harvard Business Review Press, 2008); J. M. Kouzes and B. Z. Posner, *The Leadership Challenge* (New York: John Wiley & Sons, 2006).

6. S. Oreg et al., "An Affect-Based Model of Recipients' Responses to Organizational Change Events," *Academy of Management Review* 43, no. 1 (2018): 65–86.

7. S. D. Friedman and A. Westring, "Empowering Individuals to Integrate Work and Life: Insights for Management Development," *Journal of Management Development* 34, no. 3 (2015): 299–315.

8. C. Dweck, "What Having a 'Growth Mindset' Actually Means," *Harvard Business Review*, January 13, 2016, https://hbr.org/2016/01/what-having-a-growth-mindset-actually-means.

9. Amabile and Kramer, "The Power of Small Wins"; R. E. Boyatzis, "An Overview of Intentional Change from a Complexity Perspective," *Journal of Management Development* 25, no. 7 (2006): 607–623.

10. S. Coontz, "For a Better Marriage, Act Like a Single Person," *New York Times*, February 10, 2018.

11. J. R. Edwards and N. P. Rothbard, "Mechanisms Linking Work and Family: Clarifying the Relationship between Work and Family Constructs," *Academy of Management Review* 25, no. 1 (2000): 178–199.

12. There is a plethora of new work emerging on this issue in response to what has become a crisis of attention, including C. Newport, *Digital Minimalism: Choosing a Focused Life in a Noisy World* (New York: Portfolio, 2019); and A. Alter, *Irresistible: The Rise of Addictive Technology and the Business of Keeping Us Hooked* (New York: Penguin Press, 2017).

13. J. Schmerler, "Q&A: Why Is Blue Light before Bedtime Bad for Sleep?" *Scientific American*, September 1, 2015, www.scientificamerican.com.

14. D. Goleman, "The Focused Leader," *Harvard Business Review*, December 2013, 50–60.

15. A. M. Slaughter, *Unfinished Business* (New York: Random House, 2015).

16. Friedman, *Total Leadership*.

Chapter 8

1. From a subset of the data described in S. D. Friedman and A. Westring, "Empowering Individuals to Integrate Work and Life: Insights for Management Development," *Journal of Management Development* 34, no. 3 (2015): 299–315.

2. Friedman and Westring, "Empowering Individuals to Integrate Work and Life."

3. G. Nash, "Teach Your Children," *Déjà Vu,* recorded in 1970 by Crosby, Stills, Nash & Young, Atlantic Recording Corp.

4. D. Wallace-Wells, "Parenting the Climate Change Generation," *New York Magazine*, December 20, 2018.

5. H. Sened et al., "Empathic Accuracy and Relationship Satisfaction: A Meta-analytic Review," *Journal of Family Psychology* 31, no. 6 (2017): 742–752.

Index

Acknowledgments

This book was a labor of love. And, like the labors of parenting, it was exhausting and joyful. We were immensely fortunate to have the support of wonderful people who believed in our mission and made it possible for us to carry on as we tired and to savor the good stuff.

To generate the insights, activities, and stories in this book, we undertook a yearlong research project working with parents around the country. We could not have launched such an intensive, extensive, and interactive process without the support of Michelle Rajotte—the Wharton MBA alumna par excellence, mother, military veteran, and friend who directs our company's client services and technology solutions. This book would not have been possible without her because she organized virtually all aspects of our research and brought her keen insights to the design, delivery, and analysis of our program with honesty, compassion, and tireless diligence.

The parents who participated in our research embraced it with commitment, engagement, and vulnerability—despite the demands of their busy lives. Their stories of transformation inspired us, and their feedback richly informed our thinking from beginning to end. For their willingness to take a leap of faith and join us on this journey, we are grateful to Amanda Abrams, Jill Ahluwalia, Sid Ahluwalia, Sonu Ahluwalia, Harry Allen, Herodia Allen, Anat Bujanover, Ran Bujanover, Daniel Chen, Tiffany Chu, Lisa Chung, Jason Collier, Anoop Dawar, Adrienne Demory, Greg Demory, Ben Dorfman, Gina Ferretti, Kimberly Fitch, Alex Fridlyand, Karin Fronczke, Matthew Fronczke, Griffin Gappert, Dana Garcia, Jaime Garcia, Helena Gardner, Sean Gardner, Fred Ginnebaugh, Seb Goodwin, Anjana Harve, Rohit Harve, Heidi

Hess von Ludewig, Maia Hightower, Ruth Ann Hudson, Subu Jayaram, Michael Kanaley, Despina Kontos, Abi Mandelbaum, Blaine McLaughlin, Inigo Merino, Tara Merino, Pooja Mittal, Amber Murayi, Rev Murayi, Lauren Nunnally, Christine O'Boyle, Joseph O'Boyle, Holly O'Dell, James Proulx, Jessica Ross, Kavita Sharma, Raghav Sharma, Michelle Strulovic, Stefanie Stuart, Walter Stuart, Sowmya Subramanian, Liz Tammaro, Shawn Tammaro, Lauren Tanzer, Matthew Tanzer, Eva Wang, Blaise Warren, Sarah Warren, Keith Winter, Bryan Wong, and Yating Wong. We are especially grateful to Marc Alfarano, Lucia Bonilla Fridlyand, Loretta Chen, Wes Chou, Laura Rivera, and Ann Thomson for not only participating in our research but also reviewing an earlier version of the manuscript.

We thank our colleague Scott Behson, who provided well-informed and very useful feedback on that earlier version, and the anonymous reviewers for their helpful ideas. We owe thanks to alumni of the Total Leadership course at Wharton who gave us invaluable critiques on the manuscript: Khurram Agha, Madhuri Alahari, Will Evans, Fred Ginnebaugh, Rita Jew, Michelle Leff, Ross Lucas, Natalie Mao, Abhishek Prakash, and Heather Wilkens. We much appreciate the contribution of their ideas and the instructive literature review Eric Bundonis produced while he was a Wharton student.

Melinda Merino and Kevin Evers, our editors at Harvard Business Review Press, saw the need for this book and trusted us to carve out a niche at the intersection of leadership and parenthood. We are deeply grateful to have had the gift of their unrelenting enthusiasm and guidance throughout, as we are for the remarkably resourceful and supportive Jim Levine, our literary agent, who enabled this partnership and, with graceful diplomacy, helped us break through the few logjams we encountered along the way.

Constance Hale, the writing master, sharpened our writing, refined our tone, and helped us merge our styles. She was there to kindly point out when our ideas were "stupidly obvious" and to orient us to the diverse needs, values, and experiences of our readers. Her guidance, was, as it had been on both of Stew's prior HBR Press books, indispensable.

Most of all, we thank our respective partners in parenting, Hallie Boorstyn Friedman and Dylan Lenard Westring, for making it all happen, with love.

About the Authors

STEWART D. FRIEDMAN is an organizational psychologist at the University of Pennsylvania's Wharton School, where he has been on the faculty since 1984. He founded Wharton's Leadership Program and its Work/Life Integration Project. Friedman has been recognized by the biennial Thinkers50 global ranking of management thinkers for every cycle since 2011 and was honored with its 2015 Distinguished Achievement Award as the foremost expert in the field of talent. He was listed among *HR Magazine*'s most influential thought leaders, chosen by *Working Mother* as one of America's 25 most influential men who have made life better for working parents, and presented with the Families and Work Institute's Work Life Legacy Award.

While on leave from Wharton, Friedman was the senior executive responsible for leadership development at Ford, where he created the Total Leadership program. Now in use worldwide, this program measurably improves performance and well-being in all parts of life. His research is widely cited and is included among *Harvard Business Review*'s "ideas that shaped management." He has written two bestselling books, *Total Leadership* and *Leading the Life You Want*. Winner of numerous teaching awards, Friedman inspires students' "rock star adoration," according to the *New York Times*. He advocates for family-supportive policies, serves on boards, consults with organizations, coaches individuals and groups, leads high-impact workshops, and speaks internationally. He hosts a popular show on SiriusXM's Wharton Business Radio, *Work and Life* (also available as a podcast).

ALYSSA F. WESTRING is Associate Professor of Management at the Driehaus College of Business, DePaul University. She is an award-winning educator and an inaugural Presidential Fellow at DePaul. As the Director of Research for Total Leadership, Westring brings her expertise to evaluating the impact of Total Leadership on clients and program participants. Findings from this research are used both for continuous program improvement and for disseminating the authors' discoveries and their implications for both scholars and practitioners.

Westring has coauthored many articles and chapters with Friedman and made significant contributions to the research in his books *Leading the Life You Want* and *Baby Bust*. She is also a scholar of diversity and inclusion, with a focus on women's careers in STEM fields. Her work on women in medicine has been funded by the National Institutes of Health. She is a founding member of the Research Partnership for Women in Science Careers, and her scholarly writing can be found in numerous academic journals. She regularly speaks to *Fortune* 500 companies about creating organizational cultures that facilitate work-life integration, diversity, and inclusion. She also writes for the popular press. In her TEDx talk, "The Secret Life of a Work-Life Insider," she describes how her research questions and personal journey into motherhood have shaped one another.

The Critical Skills for Integrating Work and the Rest of Life

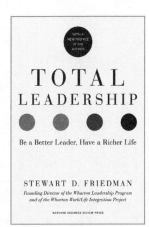

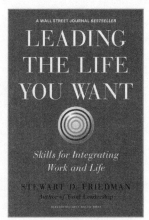

If you enjoyed reading *Parents Who Lead*, turn to these bestselling books by Stewart D. Friedman, *Total Leadership* and *Leading the Life You Want*. Together they will inspire you, inform you, and instruct you on how to take realistic steps to becoming a better leader and having a richer life.

FOR MORE VISIT STORE.HBR.ORG